University of Hull

Occasional Papers in Economic and Social History No. 4

General Editor: John Saville
*Reader in Economic History
in the University of Hull*

THE TRADE OF ELIZABETHAN CHESTER

D. M. WOODWARD

University of Hull Publications
1970

© The University of Hull 1970

SBN 90048071 8

Made and Printed in England
by Hull Printers Limited
Great Gutter Lane, Willerby, Hull, HU10 6DH

FOR MY MOTHER

PREFACE

An earlier version of this study was presented as an M.A. thesis at Manchester University in December 1965. Since then it has been substantially modified; the length has been reduced although additional material, relating especially to the trade of Liverpool, has been added. The original thesis was supervised by Professor T. S. Willan to whom I owe a great debt of gratitude for the considerable help and encouragement he has given me, both during my days in Manchester and subsequently. To John Saville I am also deeply indebted for his encouragement and advice. Two other scholars have rendered me valuable assistance; Dr. W. B. Stephens of Leeds University, who read a draft of this study and suggested certain changes, and my colleague Dr. K. R. Andrews, from whom I have learnt a great deal. However, none of these scholars is to be held responsible in any way for the inaccuracies which remain.

Like other young researchers I benefited greatly from the unstinting assistance given by archivists and librarians. Particularly I should like to express my thanks to Mrs. H. Parkinson (formerly Miss H. Boulton, sometime Chester City Archivist), Mrs. E. Berry the present Chester City Archivist, Mr. B. C. Redwood and his staff of the County Record Office at Chester, and the assistants at the Public Record Office in London. Thanks are also due to Mr. D. Waite and Mr. M. Ward of the Hull University Library for drawing the maps and to the girls of the typing pool for preparing the typescript. Finally, I should like to thank my wife who helped with the dreary round of checking typescript and proofs, assisted in compiling the index and rendered support in countless other ways.

TABLE OF CONTENTS

A NOTE ON DATING AND ABBREVIATIONS

1 All dates are old style except for the fact that the year is taken to begin on 1 January instead of 25 March. Thus what contemporaries wrote as 1 February 1568 is transcribed as 1 February 1569.

2 The following abbreviations are used in the foot notes:

A/B/1	Assembly Book, Volume 1.
A.P.C.	*Acts of the Privy Council.*
B.M.	British Museum.
Cal.	Calendar.
D.N.B.	*Dictionary of National Biography.*
E.D.A.	Enrolment Book.
F.R.	*The Rolls of the Freemen of the City of Chester*, Part 1 (ed.) J. H. E. Bennett, *Transactions of the Lancashire and Cheshire Record Society*, 51 (1906).
Harl. MSS.	Harleian Manuscripts.
H.C.A.	High Court of Admiralty.
H.M.C.	*Historical Manuscripts Commission.*
L.T.B.	*Liverpool Town Books* (ed.) J. H. Twemlow, 2 volumes (Liverpool, 1918, 1935).
M/Ap/B	Mayors' Apprentice Book.
M/L	Mayors' Letters.
M/MP	Mayors' Military Papers.
Morris	R. H. Morris, *Chester in the Plantagenet and Tudor Reigns* (Chester, 1893).
P.R.O.	Public Record Office, London.
R.O.	Record Office.
S.P.	State Papers.
S.P.D.	State Papers Domestic.
W.C.	Contested Wills.
W.S.	Wills Supra.
Wilson I	K. P. Wilson, 'The Port of Chester in the Later Middle Ages', Unpublished Ph.D. Thesis (Liverpool University, 1965), Volume 1.
Wilson II	K. P. Wilson, 'The Port of Chester in the Fifteenth Century', *Transactions of the Historic Society of Lancashire and Cheshire*, 117 (1966), pp. 1-15.

I

INTRODUCTION

Although Chester was the most important port in the north west throughout the sixteenth century it carried only a small percentage of the country's trade. Compared with London, which controlled over half of England's overseas trade, Chester was an insignificant port and many other provincial ports, or outports as they are often called, were more important. According to a detailed list of the customs paid in 1594–5 the "Port of Chester" was ranked twelfth out of eighteen outports.[1] Similarly Chester possessed only a small proportion of the country's shipping. A list of ships was compiled in 1560 and revealed that Chester possessed only two of the country's seventy-six ships of a hundred tons and over.[2] By 1582 the situation was even worse; Chester no longer possessed any of the larger vessels and had only thirteen of the country's 1,383 ships of less than eighty tons.[3] Thus from a national point of view it mattered little whether Chester's trade prospered or declined, although locally it was of considerable significance. Trade was one of the foundations of Chester's prosperity; it provided a good living for a small group of wealthy merchants and work, both directly and indirectly, for a

---

[1] *H.M.C. Cal. of Salisbury MSS.*, V (1894), p. 393. Above Chester were Exmouth, Sandwich, Poole, Hull, Ipswich, Plymouth, Bristol, Southampton, Newcastle, Chichester and Yarmouth; below were King's Lynn, Boston, Milford, Cardiff, Gloucester and Bridgwater. The "Ports" referred to in this list were not individual towns but groups of towns gathered together under the name of a head port; thus, for administrative purposes, Chester was the head port of a north-western region which included the Welsh ports north of Cardigan Bay and the Lancashire ports as far north as Grange.

[2] P.R.O. S.P.D. 12/11/27. Details for Bristol, Somerset, Carmarthen, Cardigan, Caernarvon, Anglesey, Merioneth, and Glamorgan were not given. Just over 7,000 mariners were said to live in the outports of whom 74 were from Chester and 61 from Liverpool.

[3] P.R.O. S.P.D. 12/156/45. In addition it was estimated that the country contained 1,488 ships' masters, 11,515 seamen, 2,299 fishermen and 977 wherrymen. Of these, 14 masters and 112 seamen were from Chester and the Dee. Professor Davis has shown that the great expansion of the English mercantile marine during the two decades before the Armada by-passed the north west. He estimates that in 1582 the north west owned only 2·1% of the country's shipping compared with London's 18·7%, south west 20·9%, East Anglia 27·1%, south east 16·2%, north east 15%. R. Davis, *The Rise of the English Shipping Industry in the Seventeenth and Eighteenth Centuries* (1962), pp. 1–2, 33.

sizeable proportion of the city's labour force.[1] Similarly the port provided a valuable service for the surrounding counties by acting as an outlet for some of their products and by providing them with goods which could not be produced at home.

Perhaps the greatest of Chester's disadvantages as a port was its poor location for trading with England's major overseas markets; for trade with the Low Countries and other areas in north-western Europe Chester had no advantages. For trade with southern Europe Chester was quite well located compared with the ports of eastern England but was unfavourably situated compared with the ports of the south and south west. Only for the Irish trade was Chester ideally situated; this trade was the staple trade of the city but Anglo-Irish trade was a relatively unimportant branch of England's trade during the sixteenth century. Another disadvantage was that Chester's hinterland was neither heavily populated nor industrially prosperous; there were no centres of great wealth, no flourishing industrial towns or cities, only prosperous market towns.[2] To add to this difficulty was the growth of Liverpool as a trading centre; although the development of the two ports was complementary to a certain extent the merchants of Chester were often competing in the same markets as their Liverpool counterparts. Both ports also suffered in that the expansion of the Lancashire textile industry failed to stimulate their export trades to any significant extent; by far the greatest proportion of Lancashire cloth which was destined for continental markets was carried overland and shipped from London.[3]

From at least as early as the fourteenth century Chester was battling against the ruin of its harbour facilities due to the silting up of the river. During the sixteenth century the city authorities tried to improve the facilities offered to ocean-going vessels by constructing a quay or haven, known as the New Haven, at Neston some ten miles downstream from Chester. This project was begun in the

---

[1]For a discussion of the connexion between the import of skins from Ireland and the Chester leather industry see D. M. Woodward, "The Chester Leather Industry, 1558–1625", *Transactions of the Historic Society of Lancashire and Cheshire*, 119 (1968), pp. 65–111.

[2]The same was true of Southampton's hinterland during the sixteenth century. J. L. Wiggs, 'The Seaborne Trade of Southampton in the Second Half of the Sixteenth Century', Unpublished M.A. Thesis (Southampton University, 1955), pp. 1 & 44. Exeter, which was a more prosperous port than either Southampton or Chester, tapped a prosperous industrial hinterland. W. B. Stephens, *Seventeenth Century Exeter, A Study of Industrial and Commercial Development, 1625–1688* (Exeter, 1958), p. xix.

[3]See below, p. 43

reign of Henry VIII but probably was never completed; it seems to have been nearly finished by 1569 but there were frequent references to its decayed state throughout the remainder of Elizabeth's reign.[1] It is impossible to say what proportion of goods, imported and exported through Chester, were loaded or unloaded at the New Haven, at Chester itself, or at other places. Perhaps the majority of ships, and especially the larger ships engaged in the continental trade, anchored downstream and transferred their cargoes into lighters; a petition of the Chester merchants and citizens to the privy council stated that because of inadequate harbour facilities ships were forced to "ryde now in the open rode, xvj or xxtie miles frome Chester, in great extremities".[2] Many of the troops, and much of the food and other supplies, that were sent to Ireland were gathered together at Chester, especially during the campaigns of the 1590s and early 1600s against Tyrone. From Chester the troops and supplies were sent either to the Mersey or down the Dee to be loaded aboard ships anchored off Hilbre rather than at the New Haven.[3]

As at many other ports, certain local duties were levied on the trade passing through Chester. These duties, which were laid down in a schedule drawn up in the 1530s, were paid to the Chester sheriffs, muragers, levelookers and recorder but, apart from one small duty payable to the sheriffs, the Chester freemen were exempt.[4] The existence of these duties caused some temporary, and perhaps permanent, damage to the city's trade. In 1550 the mayor of Dublin wrote to the mayor of Chester to complain about increases in the level of the duties; he expressed the hope that no offence would be taken if the Dublin merchants sought "their advantage in els wher as they do se good".[5] This breach was closed before the start of Elizabeth's reign, and it is unlikely that the Chester duties

---

[1] E. Rideout, "The Chester Companies and the Old Quay", *Transactions of the Historic Society of Lancashire and Cheshire*, 79 (1928), pp. 141–74; E. Rideout, "The Account Book of the New Haven, Chester, 1567–8", *ibid.*, 80 (1929), pp. 86–128.

[2] P.R.O. S.P.D. 12/150/36.

[3] See for example P.R.O. S.P.D. 12/252/11, S.P. Ireland 63/188/16 and many other references in S.P. Ireland. Hilbre is the name of a small, uninhabited island at the mouth of the Dee on the Wirral bank.

[4] Chester R.O. A/B/1/fos. 41–7. The two levelookers were elected annually by the city council and were officials of the Chester Gild Merchant which, by the sixteenth century, was synonymous with the whole body of freemen. See Wilson I, pp. 35–78 for a full discussions of the Chester customs down to the mid sixteenth century.

[5] Chester R.O. M/L/5/1.

depressed trade to any significant extent. Even by comparison with the national duties, which were low for most commodities, the local duties were not high; in January 1593 Robert Moore, one of the Dublin merchants, imported some beef, tallow and sheepfells on which he paid 4s. 9d. in local duties and 9s. 9½d. to the Queen.[1]

There was never any possibility of Chester becoming as large a port as Hull or Bristol but growth was possible within modest bounds. Chester's trade expanded considerably under the early Tudors and although at the start of Elizabeth's reign the level of wine and iron imports was lower than during the 1520s and 1530s it was higher than at any time during the fourteenth and fifteenth centuries. Also, by the 1560s the Irish and coasting trades were more extensive than ever before.[2] During Elizabeth's reign Chester's trade with the continent was maintained, despite serious difficulties, while the Irish trade grew to levels undreamed of by earlier generations.

---

[1]Chester R.O. Sheriffs' Customs Entry Books, 14, 1592–3 & P.R.O. E.190/1326/6.
[2]Wilson I, pp. 137–8, 168.

2

THE IRISH TRADE

XCEPT during the first decade or so of Elizabeth's reign, trade
with Ireland formed the backbone of Chester's overseas trade.
Details given in the 1565–6 port books suggest that some
two-fifths of Chester's exports by value and just over a quarter of
her imports were going to and coming from Ireland.[1] By 1582–3
about a third of Chester's imports by value were coming from Ireland
and about three-quarters of the port's exports were going to Ireland
while the relative positions in 1592–3 were two-thirds of the
imports and nine-tenths of the exports.[2] These port books, and
the information that can be derived from other port books which do
not give the value of cargoes, show that the basic structure of
Chester's Irish trade changed during Elizabeth's reign. Throughout
the late middle ages the balance of trade between Chester and
Ireland was firmly tilted in Ireland's favour[3] and this was still the
situation at the beginning of Elizabeth's reign as is shown by the
1565–6 port books. By 1582–3 however, and perhaps during the
1570s, the balance of trade had swung firmly in Chester's favour.
During the next two decades the Irish trade continued to expand
with exports to Ireland galloping ahead of imports.

Both Chester and Liverpool were well placed for trading with
Ireland and, more especially, for trading with Dublin and ports
further north. Liverpool had an advantage over Chester in being
slightly nearer to Dublin and the more northerly ports of Ireland

---

[1]Details of the commodities of trade, merchants, ships etc. in this monograph are
drawn from the P.R.O. Exchequer, King's Remembrancer Port Books (E.190)
and Customs Accounts (E.122), and the Sheriffs' Customs Entry Books preserved
at the Chester R.O. (S.C.E.) Full details of these sources are given in Appendix
III (i) and will not be repeated in the text unless the source is unclear.

[2]The Official Values of Commodities in Chester's Irish Trade (to the nearest £).

	Imports from Ireland	Exports to Ireland
	£	£
1565–6	535	360
1582–3	1,077	3,767
1592–3	2,169	9,365

These data give only a rough indication of the importance of the different
branches of the trade. The port books give the *official* values, which were laid
down in the *Book of Rates*, and not the *market* value of the goods. See T. S.
Willan (ed.) *A Tudor Book of Rates* (Manchester, 1961).

[3]Wilson I, p. 83.

and also in being nearer to the cloth-producing areas of Lancashire. In addition water transport was available for at least a part of the journey into Liverpool's main industrial hinterland. Chester, on the other hand, had the advantage of being more accessible from London and the Midlands, an advantage which was increased during the sixteenth century by the poor condition of many roads. This meant that goods carried overland from London and all areas south of Chester would tend to be exported to Ireland through Chester rather than through Liverpool. Chester also had the advantage of being a considerably larger town than Liverpool with more shops, more retailers and more craftsmen, all features which would attract merchants who wanted to build up a miscellaneous cargo for shipment to Ireland.

Such considerations will largely explain the different roles played in the Irish trade by the ports of Chester and Liverpool during this period. Liverpool was the more important port for handling imports from Ireland and this supremacy was based primarily on the shipment of yarn for the Lancashire linen industry. Considerable quantities of commodities were also exported to Ireland through Liverpool, but in this branch of the trade Liverpool had to play a secondary role to Chester which became of crucial importance during Elizabeth's reign in supplying Dublin and the Pale with a wide range of manufactured and semi-manufactured commodities. It is thus misleading to argue that Chester was surpassed by Liverpool in the Anglo-Irish trade before the close of the fifteenth century[1] for in the sixteenth century Chester and Liverpool played complementary roles in this trade with Liverpool emerging as the major importing port and Chester emerging as the major exporting port.

Chester's trade with Ireland flourished during the sixteenth century; the trade had expanded during the first half of the century[2] and continued to do so in Elizabeth's reign. The only serious threat to this trade came at the very end of Elizabeth's reign when the war in Ireland seems to have had an adverse effect on the volume of raw materials imported from Ireland at both Chester and Liverpool. On the other hand the increasing commitment of the English government to the quelling of Tyrone and his allies may have helped to stimulate the export of English and continental commodities, partly through the demand of the increased number of English

---

[1]C. N. Parkinson, *The Rise of the Port of Liverpool* (Liverpool, 1952), pp. 18–20.
[2]Wilson II, p. 14.

troops in Ireland and partly through the decay of native crafts and industries.[1]

I—*Imports from Ireland*

Throughout the sixteenth and seventeenth centuries Anglo-Irish trade was of a colonial nature; Ireland exported large quantities of raw materials and semi-manufactured goods to England and in return accepted a wide range of manufactured goods and some raw materials, such as coal and hops, that were not readily available in Ireland. This basic pattern of trade can be seen clearly in the trade which was conducted with Ireland through Chester during the second half of the sixteenth century; animal skins, raw wool and linen yarn being by far the most important commodities that were shipped to Chester.

TABLE 1:

The Import of Skins, Wool and Linen Yarn at Chester

	Sheep-skins	Kid-skins	Hides (dickers)[2]	Wool and Flocks (stones)	Linen Yarn (packs)[3]
1562–3	61,300	—	39	389	2½
1565–6	80,250	—	33	124	4
1576–7	115,952	—	14½	1,921	242
1582–3	56,940	—	1	236	97
1584–5	74,860	—	26½	172	62
1587	59,629	—	60	6	69
1588	42,655	—	1	4	27
1589	40,457	1,700	25	17	11
1592–3	106,386	17,600	5	3,958	89
1602–3	26,350	3,100	88½	30	107½

Many of the skins imported at Chester were probably processed in the city itself although some skins were sent to London and perhaps to other centres of leather production.[4] Throughout the sixteenth and early seventeenth centuries Chester was an important centre of the leather industry and benefited from the ready supply of raw

---

[1]See below for a further discussion of these points.

[2]A dicker here probably means ten hides.

[3]A pack weighed 4 cwt. and was officially valued at £5.

[4]D. M. Woodward. "The Chester Leather Industry", *op. cit.*, p. 71.

material imported from Ireland.[1] In addition to the skins imported
direct from Ireland some skins, of Irish origin, began to arrive at
Chester from Liverpool during the 1590s; in 1592–3 38,650 sheepskins were carried to Chester from Liverpool and such shipments
became a fairly regular feature of the coasting trade between the
two ports in the later 1590s and first few decades of the seventeenth
century.[2]

TABLE 2:

The Import of Skins, Wool and Linen Yarn at Liverpool[3]

	Sheepskins	Calfskins	Wool and Flocks (stones)	Yarn (packs)
1565–6	37,500	6,480	630	356
1569–70	18,650	3,200	546	66
1572–3	46,620	9,150	338	209
1573–4	47,500	9,300	380	198
1575–6	67,900	8,600	668	119
1579–80	95,550	8,400	2,411	524
1582–3	69,800	6,050	1,247	424
1584–5	58,560	7,550	70	422
1588	34,140	4,302	0	843
1589	74,450	8,350	0	1,216
1592–3	105,000	3,850	2487	1,488
1593–4	154,800	8,400	1,506	1,555
1597–8	51,050	6,650	194	43

As can be seen from Table 2, by the late sixteenth century
Liverpool was rivalling Chester as an import centre for unprocessed
skins and was much more important than Chester as an importer
of wool and linen yarn. Much of the wool imported at Liverpool,
and perhaps at Chester also, was destined for the Lancashire
woollen textile industry. By Elizabeth's reign the local supplies of
wool in Lancashire were not sufficient to meet the growing demand
and extra supplies were being drawn from both the Midlands and

---

[1] *Ibid.*, pp. 65–8, 70–1. For a picture of the national leather industry see two articles by L. A. Clarkson; "The Organisation of the English Leather Industry in the
Late Sixteenth and Seventeenth Centuries", *Economic History Review*, Second
Series, 13 (1960–1), pp. 245–56 and "The Leather Crafts in Tudor and Stuart
England", *Agricultural History Review*, 14 (1966), pp. 25–39. In addition to the
skins listed in Table I there was a small trade in the skins of badgers, otters,
goats, martens, deer and conies.

[2] P.R.O. E.190/1326/8 & 15; Woodward, *op. cit.*, p. 71.

[3] P.R.O. E190/1323/4, 9, 12; 1324/4, 6, 9, 22; 1325/9, 17; 1326/6, 8; 1327/16;
E122/31/28–35.

Ireland, although the latter did not become of crucial importance for the Lancashire industry until well on in the seventeenth century.[1] The Lancashire linen industry had as its base the flax grown in west Lancashire but again local supplies were becoming deficient and linen yarn was imported from Ireland through Chester and Liverpool in the early sixteenth century.[2] By the second half of the sixteenth century Lancashire had a thriving linen industry with centres at Bolton, Blackburn, Preston, Burnley and Wigan and especially in the area around Manchester where there was "a highly developed industry in operation which rivalled woollen manufacture in importance".[3] It has been suggested that the Lancashire linen industry underwent a vast expansion towards the end of the sixteenth century and this suggestion is certainly supported by the great increase in linen yarn imported at Liverpool during the early 1590s.[4]

The ascendency of Liverpool in the linen yarn trade was established by the middle of the sixteenth century; as Leland had noticed, some years earlier, many Irish merchants traded with Liverpool shipping "moch yrisch yarn that Manchester men do by there".[5] It is clear that the early development of Liverpool, like the later development of the port, was linked with the growth of the Lancashire textile industry. Evidence that the linen yarn imported at Chester was also destined for the Lancashire industry can be found in the Sheriffs' Customs Entry Books. After nearly every note made concerning linen yarn imported at Chester was written either the comment "gon" or else "gon to Manchester".

Although the reserves of the Irish textile industries must have been severely strained by the export of raw materials to England a small export trade in native Irish cloth, both woollen and linen, continued throughout the reign of Elizabeth I. Various types of cloth were sent to Chester—linen cloth, friezes, caddowes or coarse coverings, blankets and blanketing, coverlets, rugs, and one of the

---

[1] P. J. Bowden, *The Wool Trade in Tudor and Stuart England* (1962), p. 71; N. Lowe, 'The Lancashire Textile Industry in the Sixteenth Century,' Unpublished M.A. Thesis (Manchester University, 1966), pp. 25–6. Some of the Irish wool imported at Chester probably found its way into Yorkshire.

[2] A. P. Wadsworth and J. de. L. Mann, *The Cotton Trade and Industrial Lancashire* (Manchester, 1931 & 1965), p. 6.

[3] Lowe, *op. cit.*, p. 73.

[4] *Ibid*, p. 92.

[5] Quoted in Wadsworth and Mann, *op. cit.*, p. 6. Yarn imported at Liverpool in 1592–3 was valued officially at £7,440 whereas total goods imported at Chester from Ireland were valued at less than £2,200. P.R.O. E190/1326/8.

most characteristic Irish products, the voluminous mantle, which was one of the most popular garments in rural Ireland and was regarded by the English as an obstacle to progress.[1]

Moderate quantities of certain other raw materials were also imported from Ireland. Tallow, both in its rendered and unrendered forms, was sent to Chester in small quantities in some years; the peak in this trade occurred in 1592–3 when about 50 cwt. of tallow were shipped from Ireland and a further 60 cwt. were carried by ship to Chester probably from Liverpool. Small quantities of timber, usually in a partially prepared state, were also sent to Chester. This timber consisted of barrel staves or boards, cloven boards and some wood which no doubt was destined to be used in the Dee "fleet" —oars, oar ends and spars. An indication of Tudor government's passion for archery is given in the 1584–5 port book which records that 200 bowstaves were shipped to Chester. Some old brass, in the form of broken pots and pans, was imported. This pure metal, which needed no further smelting or refining, was ideal for remanufacture and imports grew quite rapidly during Elizabeth's reign down to 1584–5 when about 5 tons of old brass were imported; the trade then stabilised and just over $4\frac{3}{4}$ tons were imported in 1602–3.

Fish, which has been described as the most important product of sixteenth-century Ireland,[2] was one of the chief items of import at Chester and herring was the most important fish landed. A peak in this trade was reached during the 1580s; nearly 80 tons of herring were imported in 1582–3 and over 90 tons in both 1584–5 and 1587.[3] Like many of the import trades, the herring trade declined a little towards the end of the century and at the end of Elizabeth's reign the food requirements of Chester and district were supplemented by landings of fish from other English and Welsh ports.[4] Earlier in Elizabeth's reign supplies from Ireland, together with the fish

---

[1] J. S. Black, *The Reign of Elizabeth* (Oxford, 1959), p. 473. The largest quantity of Irish cloth exported to Chester occurred in 1592–3—61 mantles, 162 caddowes, 2 coverlets, 22 blankets, 30 yards of rugs, 4,470 yards of linen cloth. In some years only very small quantities of cloth were exported.

[2] A. K. Longfield, *Anglo-Irish Trade in the Sixteenth Century* (1929), p. 41.

[3] Herrings were measured by the barrel, ton and last; 8 barrels = 1 ton, 12 barrels = 1 last.

[4] 1602–3 over 600 barrels of herrings arrived at Chester from Barnstaple and the Welsh ports of Beaumaris, Milford, Porthdinlleyn, Pwllheli, and Fishguard. In addition nearly 25,000 fish, described variously as Newfoundland fish, codfish and white fish and over 30 tuns of train oil were shipped to Chester from Barnstaple, Fowey, Plymouth, London and Workington. Not all this fish was consumed locally; 96 barrels of herrings and 5,300 fish were sent north to Liverpool, Sankey and Milnthorpe.

caught by local fishermen, were probably sufficient for the needs of Chester and its hinterland. Apart from the trade in herrings there was no well-established fish trade between Chester and Ireland although in most years small quantities of other varieties of fish —cod, ling, hake and salmon—were imported.

No other foodstuffs were imported from Ireland in significant quantities during the second half of the sixteenth century although small amounts of corn and beef, mostly in barrels but some on the hoof, were imported on occasion. There is little doubt that, due largely to the devastation of war, Ireland's ability to export grain was declining during Elizabeth's reign.[1] Indeed, towards the end of this period large quantities of foodstuffs, and especially grains, were shipped out of the Dee and Mersey to feed the growing English army in Ireland.[2]

The last and rather heterogeneous group of commodities imported at Chester from Ireland fall under the general heading of re-exports and the main item in this group was wine produced in France and Spain. The import of Spanish wine continued throughout Elizabeth's reign but increased during the 1580s, as tension between England and Spain grew, and continued at a fairly high level until the end of the period. Similarly some Spanish iron was imported from Ireland from the 1580s although considerable quantities of Spanish iron arrived at Chester from France during the war years.

TABLE 3:

The Import of Wine and Iron from Ireland

	1665–6	1576–7	1582–3	1584–5	1592–3	1600–1 (6 months)	1602–3
French Wine (tuns)	—	25	$\frac{3}{4}$	3	—	—	—
Spanish Wine (tuns)	$7\frac{1}{2}$	$1\frac{1}{2}$	$27\frac{1}{2}$	$13\frac{1}{2}$	16	20	$19\frac{1}{4}$
Spanish Iron (tons)	—	—	—	1	$7\frac{3}{4}$	$5\frac{1}{2}$	$12\frac{1}{2}$ (cwt.)

A number of foodstuffs produced on the continent or further afield featured among Irish re-exports to Chester. These foodstuffs included small quantities of sugar, prunes, marmalade, oranges, raisins and the occasional cargo of French salt. Other re-exports ranged from woad to alum and from soap to "Gentish" cloth.

---

[1] Longfield, *op. cit.*, p. 110.

[2] See the many instances of provisions being shipped to Ireland in the S.P. Ireland for Elizabeth's reign.

II—*Exports to Ireland*

"The importation (of Dublin) consists of mercery wares, silks, linen cloth, woollen cloth, grocery and other commodities, which the merchants of this city buy in London and Chester, and bring hither. Some other are brought from beyond seas as wines, iron, salt, etc.".[1]

The bulk of the commodities exported to Ireland from Chester were consumption goods, many of them manufactured goods. Metal and wooden goods of English manufacture and considerable quantities of cloth, both of English and continental manufacture, found a ready market in Ireland. The increasing demand for coal in Ireland was met partly by exports from the Dee. Re-exported goods from the continent, raisins, wine, currants and sugar, to name but a few, formed a conspicuous group in this sector of Anglo-Irish trade. As Elizabeth's reign proceeded the commodities sent to Ireland from Chester became increasingly diverse and numerous. In 1565-6 about fifty differently named products were sent to Ireland but by 1602-3 the number of such products had risen to just over two hundred.

It is not possible, however, to gain a clear picture of this branch of trade because many commodities were gathered together in the port books under such headings as "and other goods valued at . . .". This may mean that some commodities were exported to Ireland and never mentioned specifically in the port books, although considering the small quantities of some commodities which the customs officials saw fit to mention it seems unlikely that many commodities failed to be noted down at some time or another. The main difficulty caused by this grouping of commodities is that it is impossible to gauge the relative importance of the different goods exported, although this is probably not true for cloth exports which seem to have been noted down fully on all occasions. In 1565-6 the commodities grouped together in this fashion amounted to about thirty three per cent of the total exports from Chester to Ireland. By the 1580s there had been a substantial increase in the volume of goods exported from Chester and the relative importance of the grouped commodities was greater than ever before; in 1582-3 the grouped commodities amounted to nearly eighty per cent of the

---

[1]*Cal. of Carew Manuscripts*, VI, pp. 174-6. The opinion of Robert Cogan touching the Customs (1611). Also quoted in C. Maxwell, *Irish History from Contemporary Sources, 1509-1610* (1923), pp. 373-4.

total exports to Ireland.[1] It would seem that as the volume of trade grew the customs officials had less time to record all commodities and resorted more and more to the device of grouping together large numbers of heterogenous commodities.[2]

Cloth—ranging from the cheap and coarse cloths manufactured in the north of England to continental velvets, taffetas and silks— was the most important commodity shipped to Ireland from Chester.

TABLE 4

The Export of Cloth to Ireland from Chester (in pieces)

	1565–6	1576–7	1582–3	1584–5	1592–3	1602–3
Kersies	22½	53	30	30	20	62½
Dozens	4	—	69	36½	19	10
Straights	10	7	34	13	—	—
Friezes[3]	—	17½	15	103½	87	151
Cottons[4]	6	117 & 1050 (yards)	18	66 & 750 (yards)	81½ & 419 (yards)	198
Penistones	—	—	15	9½	20½	13¾
Bays	—	56	12½	76½	58½	9½
Shortcloth	8	52½	86¾	90	109	10½
Fustians[5]	8	32	41½	9½	2	415½
Linen cloth[6]	4	25 & 148 (yards)	19	41	155 & 285 (yards	461 & 446 (yards)

The duty paid on the cloth represented in Table 4 expanded quickly during the early decades of Elizabeth's reign and then rather more slowly down to the end of the period. In 1565–6 approximately £7 was paid in duty and this increased to nearly £40 in 1576–7, to slightly over £50 in 1582–3, to nearly £60 in 1584–5,

---

[1]Value of grouped commodities—about £120 in 1565–6, about £3,000 in 1582–3. In 1584–5 the total value of exports is not given but grouped commodities were valued at nearly £5,000.

[2]The value of grouped commodities is not given in the later port books but this remained a very common expedient; in the 1592–3 port book commodities were grouped on more than 130 occasions.

[3]Northern, Welsh and Shrewsbury friezes.

[4]Mainly Kendal cottons but also some Manchester and London cottons. It should be remembered that at this time "cottons" were woollen cloths.

[5]Called "Jean"(Genoa), Milan, "Holmes" (Ulm) and Wesel fustians.

[6]Including cambric, lawn, Holland cloth, lockram, buckram and diaper.

to nearly £70 in 1592–3 and to approximately £75 in 1602–3.[1] It is immediately obvious, however, that the relative importance of the cloths represented in Table 4 changed during the period. Of particular note was the increased export of friezes and cottons—two cloths mainly produced in the north—and fustian and linen cloth. Conversely, the number of shortcloths exported fell significantly at the very end of Elizabeth's reign. It was due largely to this single factor that the duty paid on woollen and worsted cloth exported to Ireland was rather lower in 1602–3 than it had been ten years earlier; it was only the sharp increase in the level of linen cloth exports that pushed the total duty to a higher level in 1602–3. The decline in the export of shortcloth proved to be temporary; in 1607 232 shortcloths were exported and shipments continued to grow to a recorded peak, for the first half of the seventeenth century, of 684 cloths in 1634. Similarly ,there was an increased export of most other cloths in the first few decades of the seventeenth century and particularly in the 1630s.[2]

The volume of high-quality, luxury fabrics—including taffetas, silks, velvets, satins and gold lace—which was exported also expanded rapidly during the period. Only small quantities of such fabrics were exported during the first two or three decades of Elizabeth's reign and then in 1592–3 approximately £700 worth of these fabrics, paying some £35 in duty, were shipped out of Chester. In 1602–3 the duty paid on luxury fabrics had fallen to approximately £15 but this decline was offset, in part at least, by the significant increase in the amount of canvas which was exported—from a mere 37½ yards in 1592–3 to 2,810 yards in 1602–3.[3]

Cloth was also sent to Ireland from Liverpool; indeed during the early years of Elizabeth's reign Liverpool was exporting more cloth to Ireland than was Chester. By about the mid-point of the reign, however, Chester had become more important as a cloth

---

[1] The duties given here were arrived at by taking the total of each cloth from the port books and then estimating the duty payable according to the Elizabethan Book of Rates: T. S. Willan, *A Tudor Book of Rates* (Manchester, 1961). For a discussion of the validity of using the duty payments as an index of cloth exports see W. B. Stephens, "The Cloth Exports of the Provincial Ports, 1600–1640" *Economic History Review*, Second Series, 22 (1969), pp. 229–31.

[2] W. B. Stephens ,"The Overseas Trade of Chester in the Early Seventeenth Century", *Transactions of the Historic Society of Lancashire and Cheshire*, 120 (1969), p. 25.

[3] It is impossible to say how much duty was paid on this canvas; the port books often fail to mention the particular variety of canvas involved and duty on canvas varied from approximately 1s. 6d. to 6s. 8d. per 100 yards. Willan, *op. cit.*, pp. 13–14.

exporter and, despite some expansion of cloth exports from Liverpool during the 1590s, maintained a dominant position to the end of the period.

TABLE 5:

The Export of Cloth to Ireland from Liverpool[1]

	1565–6	1573–4	1584–5	1592–3	1593–4	1597–8
Kersies	119	8	6	7	29	13
Dozens	58	34	21	29	14	2
Straights	92	82	45	27	56	12
Friezes	—	—	4	134	138	63
Cottons	81	39	161	125	171	134
Fustians	6	2	—	$3\frac{1}{2}$	2	2

The place of manufacture of the fustians exported from Chester is not certain although most of these cloths were called Milan or Genoa fustian and a few were referred to as Ulm or Wesel fustian. It has been suggested, however, that by the early seventeenth century "these locality names had lost their original significance, because Lancashire weavers were copying 'foreign' cloths".[2] Certainly the manufacture of fustians, made from a mixture of wool and cotton of linen yarn, was introduced into Lancashire, perhaps as early as the 1560s, although this branch of the industry remained quite small during Elizabeth's reign.[3] Although it is not possible to be certain, the large export of fustians through Chester and the very low level of exports through Liverpool would suggest that most of these cloths were produced either on the continent or in other areas of England and not in Lancashire. Similarly the high level of linen cloth exports through Chester and the small quantities exported through Liverpool would suggest that this cloth was produced not in Lancashire but on the continent. Indeed it has been suggested that the great expansion of the Lancashire linen industry towards the end of the sixteenth century was based on the home market at a time when foreign markets for Lancashire cloth, and for the cloth trade in general, were disrupted by war.[4]

---

[1]P.R.O. E190/1323/4, 9; 1324/6; 1325/17; 1326/6, 8; 1327/16. Only small quantities of other cloths were exported from Liverpool.

[2]J. J. Bagley, 'Matthew Markland, A Wigan Mercer: The Manufacture and Sale of Lancashire Textiles in the Reigns of Elizabeth I and James I', *Transactions of the Lancashire and Cheshire Antiquarian Society*, 68 (1958), p. 57.

[3]Lowe, *op. cit.*, pp. 167–8.

[4]*Ibid.*, p. 92. Wadsworth & Mann, *op. cit.*, p. 14.

Some of the more traditional English cloths that were exported from Chester, such as kersies, friezes and straights, were no doubt manufactured in Lancashire as well as in Yorkshire, Westmorland, Wales and other areas. Most of the cottons exported were called "Kendals" although some were said to be from Manchester. It may be, however, that some of the Kendal cottons were produced in Lancashire for by the early seventeenth century even "penistones and kendals were just as likely to have been made in an east Lancashire cottage as in Yorkshire or Westmorland".[1] By the same period the Manchester area was also providing bays for the London market[2] and it is possible that some of the bays sent to Ireland from Chester were produced in Lancashire. In addition to the cloths mentioned already, occasional consignments of "Manchester checks"[3] and "Manchester sackcloth" were sent to Ireland as well as some motley, buffin, durance, flannel and stammel.

Some ready made clothing was also exported to Ireland. Hats of various kinds, usually called "felts", were the most important items in this trade and there was also a fluctuating trade in woollen and worsted stockings.[4] Other items of clothing included silk and velvet girdles, silk hose, cloaks, doublets, breeches, garters and small quantities of thread, buttons, lace, ribbons and sewing silk. Finally the various leather crafts of Chester found a small market in Ireland. A few dozen pairs of gloves were exported in most years as were purses, some of which were specifically called "Chester purses". Small quantities of leather points and girdles were also exported.

Throughout the sixteenth century coal, which was coming into wider domestic and industrial use, was by far the most important bulk commodity shipped out of both the Dee and the Mersey.

---

[1]Bagley, *op. cit.*, p. 57.

[2]Wadsworth and Mann, *op. cit.*, p. 13.

[3]Checks was one of the new cloths produced in Lancashire from a mixture of linen and cotton yarn. Lowe, *op. cit.*, p. 168.

[4]The peak in these trades was reached in 1592–3 when 443½ dozen hats and 132⅔ dozen pairs of stockings were exported.

TABLE 6:

The Export of Coal to Ireland from Chester and Liverpool
[in tons except where given in cauldrons (c)][1]

	1565–6	1569–70	1573–4	1576–7	1582–3	1584–5	1585–6
Chester	83	N.D.	N.D.	174	0	101	240
Liverpool[2]	247	345	114	N.D.	229	158	N.D.

	1588	1589	1592–3	1593–4	1597–8	1602–3
Chester	76	82	132c	N.D.	N.D.	11 & 454c
Liverpool	439	533	616	509	310	N.D.

It seems likely that the coal which was shipped from the Dee came
from pits close to the Welsh shore of the estuary, and especially from
Mostyn in Flintshire, rather than from the pits at Ewloe and Hawarden which were nearer to Chester.[3] In January 1597 James Ware,
an official of the Lord Deputy of Ireland, wrote to the mayor of
Chester and asked him to load two ships with coal from Mr.
Thomas Mostion for, he said, "we ar altogeather destytute of
coale". Later in the same month a certain "Gryfyth ap Robert"
wrote to tell the mayor that he had laden 20 tons of coal from the
works at Mostyn aboard the *William* of Chester for the use of the
Lord Deputy.[4] Throughout Elizabeth's reign the bulk of the coal
shipped to Ireland from the Dee remained in the control of the
masters and owners of the ships concerned; only occasionally was
coal shipped by a merchant who had no interest in the ship that
was being used.[5] This would suggest that the masters of ships

---

[1] During the sixteenth century the Chester cauldron was between 1¼ and 1⅓ tons.
In the early seventeenth century, however, Chester began to use the Newcastle
cauldron of 2 tons. J. U. Nef, *The Rise of the British Coal Industry* (2 Vols., 1932),
2, p. 370. If the Newcastle cauldron were in use in 1602–3 more than 900 tons
of coal were exported from the Dee. Note that the customs officials made no
reference to coal being shipped to Ireland from Chester in 1582–3. This may
mean that they decided to exclude coal exported to Ireland from their entries
for that year.

[2] P.R.O. E190/1323/4, 9, 12; 1324/6; 1325/9, 17; 1326/6, 8; 1327/16. E122/31/28–
35.

[3] It has been suggested that by the sixteenth century the Ewloe pits were not
producing much coal. H. J. Hewitt, *Mediaeval Cheshire* (Manchester, 1929), p. 126.

[4] Chester R.O. M/L/1/118, M/MP/8/71. In July 1600 a ship arrived at Beaumaris
carrying 24 tons of coal from "Moston pitts". E. A. Lewis, "The Welsh Port
Books 1550–1603", *Cymmrodorion Record Series*, No. XII, (1927), p. 290.

[5] The ships engaged in this coal trade were not true "colliers" but ordinary merch-
antmen occasionally carrying other commodities along with coal on the same
voyage.

called in at Mostyn, and perhaps at other creeks, to collect a cargo
of coal and carry it to Ireland at their own adventure. Had the
coal been collected at Chester it is likely that the merchants proper
would have gained control of this trade.

Some raw materials for Irish metal workers were exported from
Chester. Iron was shipped in increasing quantities down to the
middle of Elizabeth's reign but, as we have seen, during the war
against Spain the trend was reversed and Spanish iron arrived at
Chester from Ireland. At the very end of the reign a small amount
of iron was being shipped from Chester again. Small quantities of
tin, produced in Devon and Cornwall, were also shipped, as was a
little lead. Lead, most of which was probably produced in Flintshire, was not always available at Chester in sufficient quantities
to meet demand; in 1581, when some lead was required for the
Queen's service in Ireland, the mayor of Chester wrote to tell
Burghley that he could provide only two fothers of lead from
Flintshire and that even this small amount was not completely
smelted.[1] Finally small amounts of pewter and steel were occasionally
shipped to Ireland.

TABLE 7:

The Export of Metal and Metal Products to Ireland

	1565–6	1576–7	1582–3	1584–5	1592–3	1602–3
Iron	0	6 tons	26 tons	21 tons	—	12 tons
		1½ cwt.	7 cwt.	2 cwt.		
Tin (cwt.)	0	23	10	16½	60¼	6
Knives (gross)	4½	40	25	1	85	101
Nails[2] (barrels)	0	5½	2½	1	1	7¼
(nos.)	0	29,000	20,000	57,000	150,000	478,300

That Ireland was by no means self-sufficient in the manufacture
of metal wares is demonstrated by the flourishing export trade in
knives and nails. A wide variety of knives was sent to Ireland,
ranging from paring knives to pocket knives and from mincing
knives to carving knives, but most were referred to simply as
"cutts" or rather "Hallamshire cutts", that is knives made in the
Sheffield region. Various other bladed tools and weapons, including

---

[1]P.R.O. S.P.D. 12/150/4.

[2]Unfortunately the port books provide little indication of where these nails were
made. The only hint that they were produced in the Midlands occurs in the
1602–3 port book which records that William Lege of Coventry exported,
among other things, a quarter barrel of great head nails.

sickles, scythes, sword blades and daggers, were sent to Ireland in small quantities. Small quantities of other metal goods destined for both domestic and industrial use were also shipped across the Irish sea; these included hoops, hand irons and hinges as well as spades, saws, salts, shovels, snaffles, spurs and stirrups.

Three more bulk commodities, soap, salt and hops, were shipped to Ireland from Chester.

TABLE 8:

The Export of Soap, Salt and Hops to Ireland

		1565–6	1576–7	1582–3	1584–5	1592–3	1602–3
Soap	—firkins[1]	37	125	177	105	53	242½
	—cwt.	1½	8½	—	—	½	½
Salt	—tons	—	14	—	21½	18	23½
	barrels	—	266	135	287	44	200
Hops	—tons	2	8	7	23	14	4
	—cwt.	5¾	7½	15¾	12¼	10½	18¾

Much of the soap was described as "Flemish soap" although small quantities of white Castile soap were also exported. Hops, which are said to have been brought to England at the time of the Reformation and were first grown in Suffolk, Kent, Surrey and Essex,[2] were shipped to Ireland throughout Elizabeth's reign. Perhaps the main demand for hops and beer came from the English troops garrisoned in Ireland. If this were so it will help to explain the reduction in the quantity of hops shipped at the end of the period for in the early seventeenth century large quantities of beer were sent direct from England for the troops.[3]

It seems likely that a large part of the salt exported to Ireland was produced in Cheshire. Salt production by evaporation using the brine from inland springs had a long history in Cheshire and in the sixteenth century the industry was centred around the towns of Middlewich, Northwich and Nantwich.[4] Nantwich, lying on the London road, was a more important centre of the industry than the other two towns and it seems likely that much of the salt shipped from Chester was from this source; the only reference in the port

---

[1] A firkin of soap = 8 gallons, *O.E.D.*

[2] J. Thirsk (ed.) *The Agrarian History of England and Wales, 1500–1640* (Cambridge, 1967), p. 176.

[3] See for example P.R.O. S.P. Ireland 63/207 IV/67, 13 August 1600. Buckhurst to Cecil; 100 tuns of beer to be provided for the troops at Lough Foyle by William Cockayne and John Jolls.

[4] A. F. Calvert, *Salt in Cheshire* (2 Vols., 1915), 2, p. 597.

books which will support this suggestion occurs for 1592–3 when Thomas Halsall of Nantwich shipped three tons of black salt to Waterford. Some French salt was also re-exported to Ireland and contemporaries considered that it was superior to English salt; in 1599 two cargoes of salt from Brittany were sold in Ireland at about twenty shillings a hogshead while the price of the best "wich" salt was about fifty per cent dearer and yet was considered to be "nothing So good as British salt for Victualling".[1] Much of the salt shipped from Chester was for the herring fishermen of Wexford, Waterford and New Ross in southern Ireland. In addition some boats left the Dee with salt on board to fish for herring; for example in October 1576 the *Marten* of Neston sailed from the Dee with 7 tons of salt on board bound for "the coste of Ireland to make herrings".

Some glass, both of English and continental manufacture, was sent to Ireland from about the middle of Elizabeth's reign. Like many other trades the export of glass increased significantly towards the end of the period until in 1602–3 164 dozen and 60 "bunches" of glasses, 12 dozen phial glasses and 8 urinals, and 7 dozen looking glasses were sent to Ireland. At least some of this glass, such as the 4 dozen coarse English drinking glasses exported in 1592–3, was produced in England but some was specifically stated to be from Normandy and Burgundy.

Large quantities of wooden table ware, including wooden or treen cups, saucers, dishes and trenchers, were exported and once again this trade expanded during the reign to reach a peak in 1602–3.[2] A similar trade was the export of household pottery, especially an item referred to as "crocks". This trade reached a peak in 1576–7 when 87½ dozen crocks were exported while in other years small quantities of stone pots, "jar pots", "galley pots" and "earthen pots" were shipped.

Throughout Elizabeth's reign small quantities of paper were exported to Ireland but this trade remained insignificant until the last few years of the reign; in 1592–3, when more paper was exported than in earlier years, only 14 reams were shipped. By the early years of the seventeenth century far more paper was being exported; in the winter six months of 1600–1 38 reams were exported. Then in 1602–3 John Franckton, a Dublin printer, shipped 40 reams of

---

[1] P.R.O. S.P. Ireland 63/203/105. British here means of Brittany.
[2] In 1602–3 20 barrels and 192 gross of trenchers, 16 barrels and 2,294 cups, 300 cups and saucers and 200 dishes were exported.

printing paper, 5 reams of unbound books, 3 dozen coarse parchment skins for binding books and ½ a gross of primers to Dublin, while other merchants shipped a further 10 reams of unbound books, 40 small printed books, and 221 reams and 4 bundles of paper.[1]

A large and heterogeneous selection of commodities which defies classification and was probably produced partly in England and partly on the continent was shipped to Ireland. Woollen cards were shipped in most years as were other commodities which were probably for use in the Irish textile industries, such as alum and small quantities of some dyestuffs—green copperas, saffron and galls.[2] Some building materials, such as the 11,000 "brickstones" exported in 1592–3 or the 1,048 laths exported twenty years later, found their way to Ireland as well as the occasional shipment of lime, chalk, tar and pitch. Miscellaneous manufactured exports included bellows, stools and other items of furniture, lanterns, wooden combs, "turne taps" and starch. Finally some commodities were sent to Ireland to occupy the leisure time of the upper classes; for example, in both 1584–5 and 1592–3 1,000 tennis balls were exported accompanied in the latter year by three dozen rackets. On other occasions playing cards and playing tables "of Flanders making" were shipped, while at the very end of Elizabeth's reign small quantities of tobacco and pipes were shipped to Dublin to satisfy the newly introduced fad of smoking.

The last group of commodities shipped from Chester to Ireland fall under the heading of re-exports. Small quantities of wine were shipped in most years[3] together with some vinegar and brandy. A large number of comestibles was shipped of which the most prominent were currants, raisins and prunes.[4] Other fruits featured in this trade were small quantities of oranges, figs, and apples, perhaps of English growth. More savoury edibles included pepper, cloves

---

[1] Two interesting references concerning the shipment of books to Ireland have survived. In 1589 "tenne dozen schoale bookes valor £3" were shipped for a Dublin "scholemaister" while in 1603 "Lucuse Challenor doctor of divinitie overseer of Trinitie Colledge ner dublin" shipped 2 barrels and 1 dryfat containing books valued at £100 for the college.

[2] The peak year for woollen cards was 1592–3 when 325½ dozen were exported. In 1602–3 31 cwt. and 2 bags of alum were shipped, the only other sizeable shipment of alum took place in 1576–7 when 26¾ cwt. were shipped.

[3] The only sizeable shipment of wine occurred in 1582–3 when 16 tuns of French wine were exported.

[4] The peak in this Trade occurred in 1602–3 when 30¾ cwt. and 2 barrels of currants, 16 cwt. and 2 barrels of prunes and 27¼ cwt. and 1 barrel of raisins were shipped.

and olives while commodities aimed at the sweet tooth of Irish residents included sugar, marmalade, "comfits", preserve of cherries and "sugar kandey".[1] Finally, a number of commodities, most of which were produced overseas, can be grouped together under the heading of apothecary wares although it is not easy to decide to what use many of these commodities were put. The chief commodities in this group were aniseed and liquorice which were exported in most years and small quantities of a wide range of commodities which feature in the port books from time to time; these included sumach, madder, brimstone, nutmegs, oil of tartar, logwood, antimony and cinnamon.

III—*The direction of trade*

"Dublin . . . the Royal City of Ireland, and the most noble Mart, wherein the chief Courts of Judicature are held. The City is well walled, neatly built, and very populous".[2]

Dublin was by far the most important of the Irish ports with which Chester traded during Elizabeth's reign; by value over ninety per cent, and in some years over ninety-five per cent, of the goods shipped from Chester to Ireland went to Dublin. The predominance of Dublin was not quite so marked in the other branch of Chester's Irish trade but even so between seventy-five and eighty per cent of the goods imported from Ireland were shipped from Dublin. The importance of the Dublin-Chester trade is underlined by the details of the ports of sailing and destination given in Table 9.

A fairly regular trade existed between Chester and the towns of Wexford, Waterford and New Ross in the south east of Ireland. A wide variety of commodities was shipped to Chester from this region, but especially sheepfells and herrings.[3] Apart from salt no

---

[1]The only shipment of any size occurred in 1602–3 when 2 tons of sugar were sent to Ireland.

[2]W. Camden, *Britannia*, (ed.) E. Gibson (1695), p. 994.

[3]In 1592–3 about eighty five per cent of the herrings shipped to Chester came from these three ports.

TABLE 9:

The Direction of Chester's Trade with Ireland[1]

(a) The Port of Sailing of Ships Entering the Dee

	1565–6	1582–3	1592–3	1600–1 (6 months)	1602–3
Waterford	3	—	6	1	—
New Ross	—	1	1	—	—
Wexford	3	7	9	1	6
Dublin	27	37	49	7	33
Malahide	—	—	—	1	—
Drogheda	—	—	2	—	3
Dundalk	—	—	—	—	1
Carlingford	—	—	2	—	—
Ardglass	—	2	—	—	2
Strangford	—	1	—	—	2
Carrickfergus	—	—	2	2	4
Lough Foyle	—	—	—	5	15
Ireland	2	1	—	—	1
Total	35	49	71	17	67

(b) The Port of Destination of Ships Leaving the Dee

	1565–6	1582–3	1592–3	1600–1 (6 months)	1602–3
Waterford	—	2	11	1	—
New Ross	—	—	1	—	—
Wexford	3	2	11	1	6
Dublin	17	35	55	18	94
Malahide	—	—	—	—	—
Drogheda	—	—	1	1	3
Dundalk	—	1	—	—	1
Carlingford	—	2	1	—	—
Ardglass	—	1	—	—	1
Strangford	—	2	—	—	2
Carrickfergus	—	—	1	—	4
Lough Foyle	—	—	—	10	20[2]
Ireland	—	—	—	—	2
Total	20	45	81	31	133

[1] Occasionally trade was conducted with other Irish ports—Dungarvon 1588 and 1589, Wicklow 1588, Ballyteige 1588.

[2] Including five ships carrying provisions for the troops at Derry and other posts in the Lough Foyle area.

commodity was exported to these ports in significant quantities. Some trade was also conducted between Chester and various towns on the east coast of Ireland north of Dublin, but this trade was small even when compared with the trade between Chester and the ports of the south east.

Before the early years of the seventeenth century Carrickfergus was the most northerly Irish port with which Chester traded, but in both the 1600–1 and 1602–3 port books Lough Foyle appears prominently. Lough Foyle, situated in the extreme north of Ireland, became important because of English strategy in the war of 1594 to 1603 against Tyrone and his allies. Ulster which was Tyrone's country, and has been described as "the receptacle and very den of Rebels and devouring creatures",[1] was the major theatre of the war and it was an integral part of Mountjoy's strategy, when he became Lord Deputy of Ireland in 1600, to establish a strong garrison in Ulster.[2] On 14 February 1600 Mountjoy arrived at Chester on his way to Ireland carrying with him plans to establish a strong force in Lough Foyle in an attempt to reduce Ulster.[3] After long delays due to unfavourable weather a fleet of 69 ships carrying troops and provisions set sail from the Dee and Mersey and eventually arrived at Lough Foyle on 14 May.[4] A landing was effected the following day and the main garrison was established at a small settlement then named Derry.[5] For the remainder of Elizabeth's reign considerable quantities of provisions, and large troop reinforcements, were sent to Lough Foyle from Chester for the English troops resident in that area.[6] But besides the provision of clothing and food for the Queen's soldiers considerable quantities of commodities were moved to and from Lough Foyle by private enterprise. This development of trade with Lough Foyle, an area with which Chester did not trade previously, provides an early example of trade following the English flag, albeit in miniature.

---

[1] G. A. Hayes—McCoy, 'Strategy and Tactics in Irish Warfare, 1593–1601', *Irish Historical Studies*, 2 (1940–1), pp. 263–4. Quoting T. Blenerhasset, *A direction for the plantation in Ulster* (1610), p. 23.

[2] Hayes-McCoy, *op. cit.*, p. 269.

[3] C. Falls, *Mountjoy, Elizabethan General* (1955), pp. 117 & 130.

[4] P.R.O. S.P. Ireland 63/207 III/59–59I.

[5] Falls, *op. cit.*, pp. 130 & 134.

[6] See for example P.R.O. S.P. Ireland 63/207 III/57, 207 IV/35 and the many other references in S.P. Ireland and other sources.

The trade conducted with Lough Foyle was essentially similar to the rest of Chester's Irish trade; quantities of linen yarn, skins, fish, tallow and similar commodities were shipped to Chester and a wide range of manufactured goods, foodstuffs and raw materials, such as coal and hops, was sent in return. The only commodity sent to Lough Foyle which did not feature regularly in Chester's export trade was beer; 76 tuns and 62 tuns of beer were sent for the troops during the winter six months of 1600–1 and 1602–3 respectively.

A comparison between the Irish trade of Chester and of Bristol and Liverpool reveals that each port was fulfilling a rather different role in the Irish trade during Elizabeth's reign.

Liverpool, like Chester, traded regularly with Dublin but, unlike Chester, also maintained an important trade with Drogheda whence came a considerable proportion of the linen yarn imported

TABLE 10:

The Direction of the Trade of Bristol and Liverpool with Ireland

(a) The Port of Sailing of Ships Entering Liverpool[1]

	1565–6	1569–70	1572–3	1575–6	1579–80	1582–3	1597–8
Dublin	23	21	9	8	28	36	13
Drogheda	15	13	25	23	31	17	11
Other	4	12	10	6	6	7	9
Total	42	46	44	37	65	60	33

(b) The Port of Destination of Ships Leaving Liverpool

	1565–6	1569–70	1572–3	1575–6	1579–80	1582–3	1597–8
Dublin	19	15	10	3	13	25	19
Drogheda	10	14	16	16	27	18	11
Other	2	1	5	9	5	4	6
Total	31	30	31	28	45	47	36

[1] P.R.O. E190/1323/4, 9, 12; 1324/4, 9, 22; 1325/9; 1327/16.

(c) The Port of Sailing of Ships Entering Bristol[1]

	1570–1	1575–6	1591–2	1594–5	1598–9	1601–2
Waterford	16	6	33	25	16	6
Cork	4	2	9	6	1	3
Dungarvon	3	3	2	2	—	—
New Ross	1	2	1	—	1	—
Wexford	3	3	4	10	6	2
Kinsale	—	1	2	2	1	2
Youghall	—	2	3	16	1	1
Dublin	1	2	—	—	—	2
Other	2	1	2	5	2	1
Total	30	22	56	66	28	17

at Liverpool.[2] Bristol, on the other hand, played little part in the trade of Dublin, being concerned mainly with the trade of the southern ports from Kinsale in the west round to Wexford in the east. It has been suggested that in relation to Ireland "Bristol was playing the role of the Antwerp of the west"[3] but this was only true of the trade of southern Ireland. It was Chester, and Liverpool to a lesser extent, that played the role of Antwerp for Dublin and the Irish Pale.

IV—*Merchants in the Irish trade*

> The Dublin citizens "have the whole trade and traffic amongst themselves, no man to buy or sell within their liberties, unless he be a freeman . . . and there is neither merchandise, nor any manner of commodity . . . but they will have the whole bargain to themselves, not suffering any man that is not free, to buy for his own provision, no, not so much as a drinking glass, but it must be had from them, and by that means he shall be enforced to pay double the price."[4]

The trade between Dublin and Chester was heavily concentrated in the hands of the Dublin merchants; in 1565–6 they handled

---

[1]P.R.O. E190/1128/15, 1129/11, 1131/5, 10, 1132/8, 1133/3.

[2]Drogheda played a more important part in Chester's trade during the fifteenth century. Wilson I, pp. 93–4.

[3]T. S. Willan, *Studies in Elizabethan Foreign Trade* (Manchester, 1959), p. 84.

[4]Quotation from Barnaby Rich, *A New Description of Ireland* (1610), quoted in C. Maxwell, *op. cit.*, pp. 357–8.

more than eighty per cent of the trade and in 1592–3 they controlled more than eighty per cent of the commodities shipped to Chester and more than ninety five per cent of the commodities returned to Dublin. In 1565–6 thirty seven Dublin merchants were engaged in the trade but few were operating on a large scale.[1] By 1582–3, however, the trade was becoming more complex with sixty eight Dublin merchants participating while the numbers involved in 1592–3 and 1602–3 were 101 and seventy seven respectively.[2]

Most of the Dublin merchants traded with Chester on a modest scale; in 1592–3, for example, twenty eight merchants shipped cargoes to Dublin valued at less than £20 and twenty six merchants shipped goods that were similarly valued to Chester. At the other end of the scale the trade was dominated by a small group of wealthy merchants. In 1582–3 four of the merchants shipped goods to Dublin valued at more than £200 and five more merchants shipped goods valued at more than £100.[3] Ten years later the large merchants were even more prominent; two merchants shipped goods to Dublin valued at more than £600 and nineteen others carried goods valued between £100 and £600. However, only two merchants shipped goods valued at more than £100 from Dublin to Chester.[4] The majority of merchants who shipped goods valued at more than £100 to Dublin sent no goods at all to Chester. Some merchants from other towns in Ireland played a minor role in the Chester–Dublin trade but they were, nevertheless, often more important in this trade than were citizens of Chester.

There is little doubt that the Dublin merchants were able to dominate this trade by the use of restrictive practices at Dublin.

---

[1]The most important Dublin merchant in 1565–6 shipped 6 cargoes to Chester valued at nearly £38 and 2 cargoes to Dublin valued at over £25.

[2]The greater importance of the Dublin import trade is underlined by a study of the merchants involved.

	Number of Dublin merchants both importing and exporting	Number importing only	Number exporting only
1582–3	20	40	8
1592–3	28	54	19
1602–3	20	53	14

[3]Patrick Brown was the most important Dublin merchant in 1582–3, he shipped 7 cargoes to Dublin valued at £256 and 7 cargoes to Chester valued at £210.

[4]The most prominent merchants in 1592–3 were George Kennedy, who shipped 4 cargoes to Dublin valued at £646 and 4 cargoes to Chester valued at just over £10, and Philip Conran, who shipped no goods to Chester but goods valued at more than £600 to Dublin.

During the reign of Henry VIII the London merchants had complained that the "mayor and citizens of Dublin will not suffer them
to buy and sell without intolerable restrictions" and that they had
no more privileges "than if they were foreigners or pagans".[1]
These restrictions were listed in an ordinance of 1557 issued by
the City Council of Dublin which said that no foreigner should
sell his merchandise in Dublin except by wholesale and that only
freemen of Dublin were to be allowed to buy goods from a foreigner.[2]
At Dublin the body of freemen was known as the Trinity Gild and
in 1577 it was granted a new charter which gave members of the
Gild the right to sell wholesale, as well as retail, all merchandise,
foodstuffs only excepted, brought to Dublin by land or sea. No
person not elected to this body and no foreigner could sell or buy
goods within the city unless from or to merchants of the Gild. All
foreign merchants were obliged to carry their wares to the Common
Hall of the city and the Gild was empowered to fine or imprison
any foreign merchant committing offences against these regulations.[3]
These privileges were greater than those enjoyed by the merchants
of most English towns although at Chester, as in most other towns,
only freemen were allowed to sell by retail and all goods brought to
the city to be sold wholesale had to be exhibited in the Common
Hall.[4]

It is clear that the Dublin merchants enforced these restrictions
rigidly for in 1585 their activities were brought to the notice of the
Lord Deputy. It was reported that the merchants of Dublin "of
late have restrained all foreign merchants from traffic hither . . .
for whereas all commodities were afore brought unto them by
strangers, now nothing cometh in but of their own bringing . . .
and the merchants of Dublin bind all men to buy all commodities
of them".[5] It is possible that even without these restrictions the
Chester merchants still would have played a very minor role in the
trade of Dublin, although the eagerness of many of the small
Chester merchants and tradesmen to start trading with the Lough
Foyle area in the early seventeenth century indicates a desire to
participate more fully in the Irish trade.

[1]*Calendar of Letters and Papers, Henry VIII*, 13, part I. 1538 (1892), pp. 540–1.

[2]J. T. Gilbert, *Calendar of the Ancient Records of Dublin* (2 Vols., Dublin, 1889 & 1891),
I, pp. 456–7.

[3]H. F. Berry, 'The Records of the Dublin Gild of Merchants, known as the Gild
of the Holy Trinity, 1438–1671', *Journal of the Royal Society of Antiquaries of Ireland*,
30 (Dublin, 1901), part I, pp. 49–51.

[4]Chester R.O. A/B/1/f77 order, 20 September 1547.

[5]*Cal. of Carew Manuscripts*, II, p. 399.

The Dublin merchants enjoyed one final privilege in their own port; they paid no customs duty at Dublin but merely had to enter their goods in the port book and pay a fee of 2*d*. Even failure to make an entry in the port book went unpunished because by charter the Dublin merchants enjoyed the benefit of all goods forfeited in the city. It was alleged in 1571 that under these privileges the Dublin merchants were defrauding the Queen of custom by entering, under their own names, the goods of strangers.[1] Whether or not the Dublin merchants were called to account for these particular misdemeanours is not known, but four years later they were accused of committing similar offences at Chester and Dublin.

In January 1575 John Symcott, an official of the Queen, wrote to Burghley from Dublin to tell him that the Irish merchants were defrauding the Queen of large sums of money and that the searcher of Chester and his son were their accomplices. Symcott wanted a commission from the Queen to enable him, and a certain George Lodge, to remedy the customs.[2] Six months later there was some doubt as to whether or not the commission was to be enforced and Symcott again wrote to Burghley stressing the great frauds perpetrated by the Irish merchants who were still refusing to show their cockets at Dublin. He ended by saying that the commission "wilbe only waies to amende the Chester Custumes which is only our requestes".[3] Three days later Symcott wrote to tell Burghley that Thomas Cosgrave and another Dublin merchant, who were in London on business of their own, had written to their fellow merchants saying that for £100 or £200 they could overthrow the commission.[4] In the previous letter Symcott said that Henry Cusack alone had brought goods to Dublin from Chester worth £2,000 since Easter[5] and he claimed that Cusack paid 20 marks a year to the searcher at Chester for "winking" at his frauds, besides the money he thought Cosgrave and the other merchants paid.[6] As

---

[1] J. C. Gilbert, *A History of the City of Dublin* (Dublin, 1854), Vol. 1, pp. 356–8.

[2] P.R.O. S.P. Ireland 63/49/38. Symcott also asked for the office of Chief Remembrancer in Ireland for himself.

[3] P.R.O. S.P. Ireland 63/52/72 July 1575. Symcott had also written to Burghley in March 1575 saying that Ralph Grimsditch, the bearer of the letter, would declare to Burghley the deceits in the customs, *ibid*, 63/50/7. In October 1582 Ralph Grimsditch was the customer of Dublin, *ibid*, 63/96/33.

[4] *Ibid*, 63/52/76. In this letter Grimsditch was called the son, i.e. son-in-law, of Mr. Lodge.

[5] *Ibid*, 63/52/72.

[6] *Ibid*, 63/52/76.

Symcott said, the merchants could only want to overthrow the commission if in fact they were defrauding the Queen.

Early in August 1575 the Dublin merchants were still refusing to show their cockets or to declare their goods in detail rather than in bulk. They were also collecting money to overthrow the commission and threatened to "undo" Symcott, Lodge and Grimsditch if it were obtained. Nevertheless, Symcott pressed Burghley to implement the commission despite a threat to kill Grimsditch. Symcott, who had to contend with a lot of abuse from the merchants who he felt considered himself and Lodge as no better than "Verie Turks or Ethnickes", ended his letter by saying that without strong backing from Burghley he was "like to be crucified emonghtes them, by being but one litle David emonghtes so manye crwell Golias".[1] Whether or not this commission was implemented and what remedies were made is not known but this incident shows that the merchants of Dublin were prepared to be ruthless in order to get their own way and that the Chester searcher, like others of his profession, was capable of being "coropptyd for moneye".[2]

It was obvious that the Dublin merchants were not long in disfavour with the Queen for, as we have seen, a new Charter was granted to the Trinity Gild in 1577. Also, early in 1582, the Queen confirmed the Charter granted to Dublin by Edward VI by which the office of Admiralty was given to the mayor, free citizens of Dublin were freed from the payment of poundage at Chester and Liverpool, and the city was given the proceeds of the 4*d* duty, imposed in 1569, on every sheepskin shipped from Dublin.[3] However, all cloth shipped from Liverpool and Chester by the Dublin merchants still paid duty and the merchants tried to free themselves from this imposition also.[4] This plea was unsuccessful and by the time it was renewed in 1588 the searcher of Chester had modified his behaviour for the mayor of Dublin spoke of the "overhard" dealing of the searcher, customer and other customs officials at Chester.[5] This matter was raised again in 1591 and discussed by the privy council[6] but again, it seems, to no avail because duty was levied on all cloth exported to Ireland in 1592–3.

---

[1] *Ibid*, 63/53/3.

[2] R. H. Tawney and E. Power, *Tudor Economic Documents* (3 Vols., 1924), 2, p. 226.

[3] J. T. Gilbert, *Ancient Records of Dublin, op. cit.*, 1, pp. 36–7.

[4] P.R.O. S.P. Ireland 63/94/46, 51, 52; 63/98/31.

[5] *Ibid*, 63/135/3, 4.

[6] *A.P.C.* XXI, pp. 365–7.

It is possible that the Queen, in order to retain the loyalty of this wealthy and influential group of merchants, deliberately treated them leniently. Had strong backing been given to the Irish rebels by the merchants of Dublin the task of quelling the rebellion would have been all the more difficult. As it was, some of the Dublin merchants were probably giving aid to the rebels. Towards the end of the sixteenth century Tyrone received some supplies of arms through Chester and Liverpool.[1] In 1597 some Irish merchants were questioned at Chester concerning the shipment of arms for the rebels and the names of four Dublin merchants, John Wafer, Walter Galtram, Robert Panting and John Myles, were put forward as merchants trading in arms of some description. Stephen Cashell, an agent for Panting, was said to be in Manchester on some business and Thomas Long, another of Panting's agents, had just returned to Ireland.[2] It was not certain whether the arms taken to Dublin were for Tyrone although Thomas Long was said to have "stolen over" with muskets and a certain Nicholas Harcles was thought to have supplied all the lead required by the rebels in northern Ireland, from Manchester, for the previous two years.[3] In 1598 letters were sent to Bristol and Chester ordering that arms and munitions ready to be shipped by Irish merchants should not be allowed to go to Ireland for it was feared that these were for the use of the rebels.[4] Again in 1599 a warning was given that the rebels were obtaining arms from England which were being shipped from London, Bristol, Chester and other ports.[5] Had the Queen not been so benevolent to the merchants of Dublin it is possible that they would have indulged in gun-running and arms supply for the rebels to a much greater extent.

The merchants and tradesmen of Chester played only a small part in the trade with Ireland. Despite the restrictions placed on foreign merchants, however, Chester men maintained slender links with Dublin throughout the period but they tended to be rather more important in the trade with the other Irish ports. This is especially true of the end of the period when a number of Cestrians took part in the trade which developed with Lough Foyle. Those Chester merchants who traded with the continent had only a small

---

[1] R. Bagwell, *Ireland under the Tudors* (3 Vols., 1885), 3, p. 451.
[2] P.R.O. S.P. Ireland 63/199/107.
[3] *Ibid*, 63/199/116.
[4] *A.P.C.* XXIX, p. 244.
[5] P.R.O. S.P. Ireland 63/205/125.

interest in the Irish trade and when they did trade with Ireland it was normally either to obtain some commodity that they usually imported direct from the continent or to distribute commodities brought by them to Chester from the continent. Only occasionally did these merchants trade with ports other than Dublin and on the whole the Irish trade was left to men with smaller resources, many of whom traded with Ireland to obtain raw materials for their particular craft or, more occasionally, to obtain an outlet for their products.[1]

Merchants from various other towns and ports in England and Wales also traded with Ireland through Chester on occasion, but few showed any tendency to establish themselves regularly in this trade. One or two Lancashire merchants appear on a number of occasions but only Robert Cutt, a London ironmonger, traded regularly with Ireland. Cutt, who was Master of the London Ironmonger's Company in 1599 and 1608,[2] traded through Chester at least as early as 1560 and he continued to appear regularly in the port books and customs accounts to the very end of Elizabeth's reign. He also traded with Ireland through Liverpool in many years. Cutt tended to specialise in the shipment of commodities to Ireland and 1584–5 was one of his most active years, when he shipped 44 cwt. of hops, 19 firkins of soap, some steel and various other commodities. On occasion he also undertook the supply of provisions for the army in Ireland; in May 1581 Burghley received a letter from Chester which said that if some money were given to "Robart Cutt purveior of the hoppes" he would see that the necessary provisions arrived safely in Chester.[3] A month later Burghley received another letter from Chester which informed him that Robert Cutt, who was said to live in St. Laurence Lane in London, was "dailie acquainted with the Carriages that come hither".[4]

Not all the merchants who traded with Ireland conducted their own business personally; agents or factors, acting on behalf of one or more merchants, handled rather more than a half of the goods carried to Chester and between a third and a quarter of the goods

---

[1]Chester tradesmen and craftsmen who traded with Ireland were drawn from many occupations; they included glovers, tanners, coopers, sailors, mercers, drapers, tailors, innkeepers and ironmongers.

[2]J. Nicholl, *Some Account of the Worshipful Company of Ironmongers*, (1851), p. 553.

[3]P.R.O. S.P. Ireland 63/83/33.

[4]*Ibid*, 63/83/55.

shipped back to Ireland.[1] These factors, who signed the port books in the custom house in lieu of the merchant, were drawn mainly from the commercial communities of Chester and Dublin and, to a lesser extent, from other areas in Ireland. But until Thomas Tomlinson developed his agency business into a thriving concern during the last decade or so of Elizabeth's reign none of the Chester tradesmen or craftsmen acted as factors on a permanent basis. Tomlinson, a cooper by trade,[2] acted as a factor on a modest scale in 1592–3; in that year he supervised the shipment of ten cargoes valued at about £112 that were sent to Ireland and received one cargo in return, valued at nearly £2. By 1600–1 his trade had become more organised and in the winter six months covered by the port book he acted as factor for fifteen cargoes shipped to Ireland valued at £220, although the goods imported under his supervision were valued at less than £1. Two years later, in 1602–3, Tomlinson's factorage business had grown into a thriving concern. Unfortunately no values are given in the 1602–3 port book but the growth of his importance as a factor is undoubted; he supervised the shipment of only a small quantity of goods imported at Chester but acted as factor for sixty one cargoes belonging to thirty two merchants that were returned to Ireland. These cargoes included more than seventy different commodities ranging from 41 cwt. of hops to 20 cwt. of alum, from 68½ firkins of soap to 16 cauldrons of coal, and from 174 dozen glasses to 44 reams of paper. Cloth was the most valuable commodity that he shipped to Ireland; in 1602–3 he controlled the shipment of 51 pieces of fustian, 143 pieces of lawn and cambric, 10 friezes, 13 kersies, 53 Kendal cottons, 10 Manchester cottons, 94 pieces of Holland cloth and 3¾ pieces of short cloth.

Unfortunately it has not been possible to discover anything further about the organisation of Tomlinson's business and the reward that he received from his clients; whether or not he received the 2½ per cent commission which may have been the customary rate for factors in Europe during this period[3] is not clear. Whatever his reward, however, he was not a very rich man, although he probably lived in a relatively comfortable fashion compared with many Elizabethan craftsmen. At his death in 1611 he occupied a house of eight rooms, including lofts, kitchen and buttery, which contained goods valued at £51 8s. Tools and materials necessary to his trade

---

[1]Based on details derived from the 1565–6, 1582–3, and 1592–3 port books.
[2]*F.R.*, p. 63
[3]Willan, *op. cit.*, p. 30.

as a cooper were valued as £24 5s 7d., and his total assets, including his cow which was valued at £3 and the lease of a house and cellar in Watergate Street worth £17, amounted to £95 13s 7d.[1]

Various factors who came over from Ireland were more important than the Chester factors and the majority of the Irish factors were not merchants in their own right but either apprentices or servants of the merchant for whom they were acting. In most cases these factors, who did little or no trading on their own account, worked for one merchant only and presumably returned to Ireland when the particular job in hand was completed. Such factors were responsible for cargoes of all sizes and values; at the one extreme they shipped cargoes valued at less than £10 while at the other extreme were the two cargoes shipped by Robert Kennedy, for Philip Conran of Dublin, in 1592–3 which were valued at £623 15s. Despite the widespread use that was made of factors, however, many of the Dublin merchants came over to Chester to handle their own cargoes. They made the sea crossing to deal with cargoes ranging from the very small to the very large, although there was a tendency among the more prominent merchants to supervise personally the shipment of a valuable cargo and leave the supervision of smaller cargoes to a factor. Another business technique employed by the Dublin merchants on occasion was for one of the established merchants to act as a factor for one or more of his brother merchants during a visit to Chester.

The Chester merchant community derived only a small direct benefit from the trade with Ireland but this does not mean that Chester and her citizens received no benefit from the trade. The city authorities gained by the local duties levied on many of the goods carried to and from Ireland, some of the city's craftsmen, and especially the leather workers, benefited by drawing part of their raw materials from Ireland, and many retailers and craftsmen must have gained considerably by selling their wares to the Irish merchants. That Chester retained the outward appearance and trappings of a port was due in large part to the dozens of ships which annually plied across the Irish Sea.

---

[1]Cheshire R. O. W.S. 1611 Thomas Tomlinson.

V—*Postscript: The Manx and Scottish trades*

The trade conducted from Chester with Scotland and the Isle of Man[1] was on a small scale and it was essentially a miniature of the Irish trade; raw materials were the main goods sent from these areas and in return they imported manufactured and luxury wares from Chester.

There was little or no trade between Scotland and Chester during the early decades of Elizabeth's reign; there is no mention of Scotland in the 1565–6 port books and it seems unlikely that any trade was conducted with Scotland in 1576–7.[2] By 1582–3, however, a small trade had developed with this area. Imports from Scotland mainly comprised quantities of herrings and other fish and small quantities of skins, hides, linen cloth, wool and pitch. Exports were more varied ranging from cloth produced in the north of England to canvas, hats, linseed, lead, calfskins, wheat, barrel hoops and other commodities.

The various trading groups at Chester seem to have had little interest in the Scottish trade either in order to distribute their products or to obtain raw materials. Most of the trade with Scotland was due to Scottish initiative and was conducted in Scottish ships with many of the cargoes entered in the name of the ship's master. The ports in Scotland with which Chester traded were Ayr, Irvine, Glasgow and Dumbarton, all quite close to one another on the east coast.

If anything the Manx trade bore an even closer resemblance to the Irish trade. The most important imports from the Isle of Man were sheep fells, wool and hides[3] and other imports ranged from herrings and tallow to occasional shipments of small quantities of French wine, old brass, train oil, honey, tar, salt, hemp, feathers and madder. Finally some salted beef was sent to Chester in most years and occasionally some live animals such as the 12 "quick" bullocks and 10 "quick" sheep imported in 1592–3.

As in the Irish trade Chester had a considerable favourable balance of trade with the Isle of Man. The commodities sent to the Isle of Man were similar to those sent to Ireland except that the range of goods going to the Isle of Man was much narrower and

---

[1] English trade with the Isle of Man was a branch of foreign trade during this period.

[2] The 1576–7 port book does not refer to ports of destination or sailing.

[3] Peak years in these trades were 1592–3—8,080 sheepskins and 281 stones of wool 1602–3—15 dickers of hides.

did not include the more exotic and expensive commodities which featured in the Irish trade. No single commodity, or group of commodities, stands out in this trade as being worthy of special notice but the range of commodities sent over demonstrates that the Manx economy, like the Irish, was by no means self-sufficient in basic manufactured commodities.[1]

Most of the ships engaged in this trade belonged to the Isle of Man and they were for the most part very small with a carrying capacity of less than 10 tons. These ships regularly plied the route between Chester and Douglas making only occasional trips to Peel, Ramsey and Castletown.

During the early part of Elizabeth's reign this trade was concentrated largely in the hands of Manx merchants but during 1582–3, and for the remainder of the period, a number of Chester craftsmen became of some importance in the trade. One noticeable feature of the Manx trade, as distinct from the Irish trade, is the absence of factors and this suggests that the merchants involved travelled to and from Chester in order to supervise personally the shipment of their cargoes. There is some evidence to support this suggestion; Roger Darwell was ordered to appear before the Portmote Court at Chester in 1586 but failed to do so and the reason given for his absence was that he was "then in the Isle of Man the wind not servinge to Retorne".[2] It is clear that two Chester merchants were in the Isle of Man some years later for the Governor wrote to the mayor of Chester to complain about their treacherous behaviour.[3]

Compared with the total volume of trade passing through Chester the trade with Scotland and the Isle of Man was insignificant. To the men engaged in these trades it was probably not so. Some of the Chester Craftsmen traded in the raw materials which would later be processed in their workshops thus cutting out profits which would normally accrue to the middleman. For the inhabitants of the Isle of Man the trade with ports such as Chester and Liverpool was of crucial importance in supplying them with many of the necessities of everyday life and providing them with a market for their products.

---

[1]Goods shipped to the Isle of Man included salt, iron, tin, spades, nails, knives, crockery, soap, canvas, cloth, items of clothing, wool and linen cards, spinning wheels, hops, malt and barley.

[2]Chester R.O. A/B/1/f.206. The Portmote Court was a monthly court held by the sheriffs. Morris, p. 198.

[3]Chester R.O. M/MP/8/69, 1597.

3

THE CONTINENTAL TRADES

I—The trade with France and Spain

DURING Elizabeth's reign the great bulk of Chester's continental trade was conducted with France and Spain.[1] These were the most accessible countries on the continent for ports situated in the north west of England, although even in these trades Chester was much less favourably situated than the south coast ports. On the other hand the sea route from Chester to areas south of Brittany was little longer than the route from London to such areas. For other sectors of continental trade Chester was much more disadvantageously located; the voyage from Chester to the Low Countries was long while the shortest route to Scandinavia and the Baltic necessitated a difficult voyage through the dangerous waters of western Scotland.

Ships arriving at Chester from Spain came mainly from the Biscay ports of Bilbao, Bermeo and San Sebastian, and they carried a variety of commodities ranging from quite large quantities of train oil to much smaller quantities of pitch and resin, ostrich and sheep wool, and vinegar.[2] However, iron was by far the most important commodity imported from this area; this trade reached a recorded peak for Elizabeth's reign in 1562–3 when 363 tons of iron were imported.[3] Andalusia was the only other area in Spain from which goods were sent to Chester. Thus in 1565–6 one cargo comprising 15 tuns of sack, 175 pieces of figs, 30 pieces of raisins[4] and 1 cwt. of pepper, arrived at Chester from Andalusia while in 1576–7

---

[1]Chester traded with France throughout the Middle Ages but the Spanish trade was opened up only during the 1470s. Wilson II, p. 14.

[2]Train oil—1565–6 24 tuns, 1576–7 none, 1582–3 17 tuns; Pitch—maximum 1582–3 21 cwt.; Vinegar—maximum 1584–5 6 tuns.

[3]For the details of iron imports in other years see Appendix I (*a*). Spanish iron was of a good quality at this time; it has been suggested that it was preferred to German iron for agricultural purposes. It also seems that in 1569 Spanish iron was more expensive than English iron at London—Daniel Höchstetter bought 5 tons of Spanish iron for £55 and 3 tons of English iron for £28 for the Mines Royal Company. G. Connell-Smith, *Forerunners of Drake* (1954), p. 5; W. G. Collingwood, "Elizabethan Keswick", *Cumberland and Westmorland Antiquarian Society, Tract Series No. 8* (1912), p. 55.

[4]A "piece" of figs was perhaps equivalent to about 22 lbs. T. S. Willan, *A Tudor Book of Rates* (Manchester, 1961), p. 25.

a cargo of 48 tuns of sack, 1 cwt. of pepper, 1 cwt. of sugar and 15lb of cinnamon, which arrived from an unnamed port, was probably also from Andalusia. It is not possible to say with any certainty whether or not this trade between Chester and southern Spain was on a regular basis during the early decades of the reign, but it was always much less important than the trade with northern Spain.[1]

The only reference to be found in the port books, and other customs records, concerning trade between Chester and Portugal is for 1585 after Portugal had been temporarily absorbed into the Spanish Empire. In April 1585 a ship arrived at Chester carrying 32 pieces of calico cloth, 8 butts of muscatel wine, 1¼ cwt. of pepper, ½ cwt. of currants and 32 tons of salt; 8 tons of the salt were referred to as "Portingale" salt which suggests that the cargo came from Portugal. The other commodities on board were also typical products of Portugal.[2] Evidence that the Chester merchants did trade with Portugal, on occasion, can be obtained from another source; in 1578 William Pillen and other Chester merchants freighted a ship, the *Felix*, from Chester to Lisbon.[3]

Wine, which was by far the most important commodity imported from France, was shipped to Chester mainly from the ports of Bordeaux and La Rochelle and to a lesser extent from Libourne and Marennes.[4] Other commodities sent to Chester from these ports included vinegar, prunes, oranges and salt with occasional small shipments of tar, honey, turpentine, walnuts, quinces, chestnuts, alum, feathers and pepper.[5]

The outbreak of open war between England and Spain in May 1585 led to a significant change in Chester's pattern of trade with both France and Spain. Direct trade with Spain, although not

---

[1] In the late fifteenth century Chester's trade with Spain was conducted with the Biscay ports only and they remained the most important Iberian ports to trade with Chester throughout the first half of the sixteenth century despite the establishment of trade with Andalusia and Portugal in the second decade of the century. Wilson I, pp. 129–131.

[2] An undated trade manual, attributed to Elizabeth's reign, listed pepper, calico cloth and "salte of Portingall" among the goods to be brought from Lisbon. Tawney and Power, *op. cit.*, 3, pp. 199—210.

[3] P.R.O. S.P.D.15/25/95.

[4] French wine was imported at Chester from at least as early as the thirteenth century. Wilson I, p. 108. For the detail of wine imported during Elizabeth's reign see Appendix I (*a*). The great bulk of the wine featuring in Appendix I was imported directly from France.

[5] Peaks in the major of these trades; 1565–6 vinegar 7½ tuns, salt 600 barrels; 1584–5 prunes 67½cwt., oranges 50,000.

impossible during the years after 1585, became much more difficult and in the years immediately after 1585 Chester's trade with both France and Spain became rather precarious. The first response of the Chester merchants to the events of 1585 was to switch their trading activities from the Biscay ports of Spain to the port of St. Jean de Luz less than twenty miles from the Spanish frontier in the extreme south-western corner of France. From 1585 onwards all the Spanish iron which arrived at Chester direct from the continent was shipped from St. Jean de Luz. This link was forged immediately after the outbreak of hostilities in the summer of 1585; in October 1585 46 tons of Spanish iron arrived at Chester from St. Jean de Luz and a few months later in April 1586 it was believed that Richard Holker, one of the Chester merchants, had died there.[1] Various other commodities of Spanish origin, including some wool and figs, were also exported through St. Jean de Luz. The export of Spanish commodities from St. Jean de Luz stimulated the export of native French products from that port; thus in 1592–3 94 cwt. of Toulouse woad were shipped to Chester. This was not the first time that this commodity had been shipped to Chester for ten years earlier 114 cwt. of Toulouse woad arrived from Bordeaux and a further 9 baskets of woad were imported from an unnamed port in 1584–5. In addition small quantities of pitch, resin, salt and vinegar were shipped from St. Jean de Luz.

Trade between England and Spain had been increasing during the first half of Elizabeth's reign[2] so that it came as a considerable blow to English merchants when it was seriously threatened by the events of 1585. That the merchants considered the trade to be of importance and profit is demonstrated by the great efforts they made to keep it open; firstly, as we have seen, much of the trade with northern Spain was re-routed through the French port of St. Jean de Luz and secondly, despite the great dangers involved, a surprising volume of direct trade was maintained partly through the agency of foreign merchants and foreign shipping but also through English merchants and shipping. Direct trade between Southampton and Spain continued throughout the war although at a lower level than in the prewar period; in the Armada year, for example, three ships reached Southampton from Spain and Portugal and a further seven ships from the Azores, Canaries and Madeiras.[3] Similarly direct

---

[1] Chester R.O. A/B/1/f.201.

[2] K. R. Andrews, *Elizabethan Privateering 1585–1603* (Cambridge, 1964), p. 13.

[3] J. L. Wiggs, *op. cit.*, p. 81 Note also details of the maintenance of direct trade in 1593 and 1600.

trade between Bristol and Spain was maintained throughout the war[1] and three ships arrived at Exeter from Madeira or Portugal in 1597–8.[2] Towards the end of the war the direct trade between London and Spain was by no means negligible; between October 1600 and June 1601 51 ships, out of a total of 714 ships entering London were from Spanish territories.[3]

The scattered evidence which relates to the maintenance of direct trade with Spain suggests that the bulk of this trade was conducted with the ports of southern Spain and the Atlantic Islands. Even Chester managed to conduct a certain amount of trade with these areas during the war years. In March 1587 the *Lyon* of Dundee arrived at Chester from Cadiz carrying 43¼ tuns of sack belonging to three Scottish merchants from Dumbarton, Ayr and Leith.[4] Some years later, in August 1593, the *William* of Leith arrived at Chester from San Miguel in the Azores with a cargo of 20 tons of green woad and 1,500 reeds or canes belonging to Richard Bavand the younger, one of the Chester merchants.

Another way to circumvent the official stoppage of trade was to import Spanish produce from Ireland; Ireland, in theory a part of Elizabeth's kingdom, maintained direct trade with Spain throughout the war. In 1595 it was suggested that the Irish merchants were much more in evidence in Spain than their English counterparts— "The Irish have as free in Spain as ever, but not the English". It is interesting to note that the Spanish sailor who gave this evidence said that he knew of "no Englishmen in Spain, except Puddington

---

[1]Ships entering Bristol from Spain or Spanish Territory

From	1591–2	1594–5	1598–9	1601–2
Spain	3	5	10	9
Portugal	1	–	5	6
The Islands	2	4	6	3

Most of the Spanish ports were in the south; the trade with northern Spain tended to find its outlet through St. Jean de Luz. P.R.O. E190/1131/5, 10; 1132/8; 1133/3.

[2]W. G. Hoskins, "The Elizabethan Merchants of Exeter", *Elizabethan Government and Society, Essays Presented to Sir John Neale* (ed) S. T. Bindoff et al. (1961), p. 170 •

[3]L. R. Miller, "New Evidence on the Shipping and Imports of London 1601–2". *Quarterly Journal of Economics*, XLI (1927), pp. 752 and 760. There are many other references to direct trade with Spain; see for example Willan, *op. cit.*, p. 16 for details of an English factor in Spain in 1588 and A. H. Dodd, "Mr. Myddelton the Merchant of Tower Street", *Essays Presented to Sir John Neale, op. cit.*, p. 260 for details of Myddelton's trade with Spain in the 1590s. See also *Cal. S.P.D.* 1591–4 p. 284, 1595–7 p. 101, 1598–1601 pp. 66, 242–3 and A. B. W. Chapman, "The Commercial Relations of England and Portugal, 1487–1807", *Transactions of the Royal Historical Society*, Third Series, 1 (1907), pp. 161–2.

[4]P.R.O. E190/1325/21. There is no mention of this cargo in the two customs accounts which cover March 1587, E122/31/25,26.

and John Fleting of Chester or Liverpool".[1] As we saw in the previous chapter, Chester benefited from this backdoor into Spain by importing quantities of sack and Spanish iron from Ireland.

The final way for English merchants to secure Spanish and Portuguese commodities for the home market was to join in the large scale plunder of merchant shipping. Those merchants who traded with Spain were initially strongly committed to the need to maintain peace with Spain but once the war had broken out they cut their losses, moved over *en bloc* to the war party and became the chief force behind the privateering war.[2] Many of the privateers operating in the early years of the war were owned and equipped by provincial merchants, but in most cases this form of privateering proved to be unprofitable and as the war progressed the pursuit of plunder became more and more the preserve of the professionals and great merchants, with the major impetus of the campaign coming from London.[3] Only once did the Chester merchants take part in such a venture. In 1590 or 1591 the *Harry Bonaventure* of Chester, burthen about 90 tons, was fitted out with 12 guns, victualled for six months and manned by a crew of 60 to be used "in warlike manner agaynste the Kinge of Spayne and his subiectes and his or theire goodes". Henry Bedford sailed as captain and William Thornton as master.[4] Unfortunately details concerning the progress of the *Harry Bona-venture* and the success or failure of the project are not available. Henry Bedford was apprenticed to Richard Knee, one of the Chester merchants, at the time of this voyage.[5] This would suggest that Bedford was put in charge of the voyage by Knee and a group of the more important merchants.[6]

The achievement of the Chester merchants in managing to maintain the flow of Spanish commodities into the north west after 1585 is all the more significant when compared with the course of Liverpool's continental trade during the war period. The trade conducted from Liverpool with France and Spain, which had never

---

[1]*Cal. S.P.D.* 1595–7, pp. 139–40. See also 1598–1601, p. 66 and 1591–4, p. 236 for similar statements. There is no reference to a John Fleting either in the *F.R.* or *L.T.B.*

[2]Andrews, *op. cit.*, pp. 15 and 112.

[3]*Ibid*, pp. 140–1, 147.

[4]P.R.O. H.C.A. 25/3(9). I am grateful to Dr. K. R. Andrews for providing me with this reference.

[5]*F.R.*, p. 70. He became a freeman of Chester in July 1592.

[6]Because of the high cost and great risks involved in a privateering venture it is unlikely that Knee was the sole backer of the *Harry Bonaventure*.

been as important as Chester's trade with these countries during
the earlier part of Elizabeth's reign, collapsed completely after
1585; in 1592–3, 1593–4 and 1597–8 trade between Liverpool and
the continent was at a stand still.[1]

*   *   *

During the first half of Elizabeth's reign exports to France and
Spain consisted mainly of that variety of woollen cloth known as
Manchester cottons. This cloth, which was produced in a variety of
different colours, was manufactured in the Manchester area, in
Bolton and Bury and the district around Blackburn[2] and seems to
have found a ready market on the continent.

TABLE 11:

The Export of Manchester Cottons from Chester
(measured in goads[3])

	To France	To Spain	To France or Spain	Total
1562–3	—	—	16,700	16,700
1565–6	5,700	19,900	—	25,600
1576–7	—	—	12,350	12,350
1582–3	3,600	13,950	—	17,550
1584–5	—	—	10,500	10,500
1585–6	2,000	—	—	2,000
1587	400	—	—	400
1588	1,800	—	—	1,800
1589	—	—	—	—
1592–3	110	—	—	110
1602–3	—	—	—	—

From the limited amount of information available it would seem
that the bulk of the Manchester cottons shipped from Chester was
destined for the Spanish market; in 1565–6 Manchester cottons were
shipped to the Spanish ports of Vigo, Corunna, Portugalete,
Bermeo and also to Andalusia and "Biskay". In 1582–3, however,
exports were restricted to the ports of Galicia and the Biscay coast.

[1]The Import of Spanish Iron and French Wine at Liverpool

	1565–6	1569–70	1572–3	1573–4	1575–6	1579–80	1582–3	1584–5
Iron	94	178½*	59½*	50*	22½	77½	150	123½
Wine	—	—	—	—	—	—	38	34

*Imported via France

E190/1323/4, 9, 12; 1324/4, 6, 9, 22; 1325/9, 17; 1326/6, 8; 1327/16

[2]Lowe, *op. cit.*, p. 8.

[3]A goad was 1½ yards.

Exports to France went primarily to the great wine ports of Bordeaux and La Rochelle.

Smaller quantities of Manchester cottons were exported to France and Spain, and to a lesser extent to Portugal, from Liverpool; this again underlines the greater importance of Chester in the continental trade during this period.[1] However, both Liverpool and Chester were completely overshadowed by London in the export of this cloth. During the summer six months of 1576 no less than 67,154 goads of Manchester corrons were shipped from London to the continent and the greater part of these went to France with small quantities being shipped to Spain, Russia, Danzig and the Low Countries.[2]

During the second half of Elizabeth's reign tanned calfskins became the main commodity exported from Chester to the continent. This trade developed after 1584 when the Queen granted a licence to the Chester merchants to allow them to ship 10,000 dickers of tanned calfskins to the continent over a period of twelve years.[3] Before 1584 the port books record that only small quantities of leather were sent to the continent from Chester. Details from the 1584–5 port book suggest that Spain was a better market than France for tanned calfskins but the outbreak of the Anglo-Spanish conflict in the summer of 1585 left France as the sole market. However, a large proportion of the calfskins shipped to France were bound for St. Jean de Luz which suggests that some of these skins may have found their way over the frontier, or along the coast, into Spain in exchange for Spanish iron.

---

[1]For eight years (1565–6, 1569–70, 1572–3, 1573–4, 1575–6, 1579–80, 1582–3, 1584–5) about 8,100 goads of cottons were exported on average to France and Spain from Liverpool whereas during 5 years in the same period the average export of cottons from Chester was just over 16,300 goads. Liverpool references as in note 1, p. 42.

[2]Manchester cottons amounted to 43% of all cottons exported from London during that period (total export 156,161 goads). The export of cottons from London was even greater in later years although it is not possible to distinguish between Manchester and other cottons—1594–5, 168,065 goads; 1598–9 211,082 goads. Lowe, *op. cit.*, pp. 112–3, 119.

[3]P.R.O. Patent Rolls, 26 Elizabeth, part 7, mem. 1–4. A dicker here means 10 dozen or 120 skins. The history of this grant, which led to much ill-feeling at Chester, is discussed in Chapter 5.

TABLE 12:

The Export of Calfskins from Chester (in dickers)

	To France	To Spain	Total	Total in Skins
1584–5	26	113	139	16,680
1585–6	465·5	—	465·5	55,660
1587	321·5	—	321·5	38,580
1588	361·2	—	361·2	43,344
1589	247·6	—	247·6	29,712
1592–3	415·3	—	415·3	49,836
1602–3	392·7	—	392·7	47,124

It seems likely that the war with Spain had an adverse effect on the calfskin trade for the Chester merchants did not ship their quota of 833 dickers a year as allowed by their licence. Indeed, by 1598 they had shipped only some 2,906 dickers of calfskins to the continent and their licence was renewed for a further nine years to allow them to ship the remaining calfskins.[1]

Small quantities of cloth, in addition to Manchester cottons, were exported to both France and Spain. The most important year in this trade was 1587 when 22 short cloths, 103 kersies and 56 straights were sent to France. Cloth usually went to the ports of northern Spain and south west France but in 1584–5 12 friezes and 100 yards of flannel cloth were sent to Le Conquet in Brittany and to Barfleur in Normandy.[2]

The only other commodities sent to France and Spain in any sizeable quantity were coal and lead. Coal was shipped to France fairly regularly, the amount exported fluctuating between the 20 tons shipped in both 1582–3 and 1587 and the 110 tons shipped in 1585–6, while 24 tons of coal were exported to Spain in 1565–6. Lead, on the other hand, was exported only in small quantities except for a short period during the late 1580s when 131½ tons of lead were exported to France in four and a half years.[3] In addition to the commodities mentioned already, small quantities of wax, copper, herrings, barley and wheat were shipped to France and Spain on occasion.

*   *   *

[1] P.R.O. Patent Rolls, 40 Elizabeth, part 16, mem. 19–24.

[2] Other cloths sent to the continent in other years were dozens, linen cloth, Welsh cottons, bays and "Chester Russetts."

[3] 92 tons of the lead were shipped by William Massey and 20 tons by Richard Knee.

The long series of data relating to the import of wine and iron at Chester will allow us to make some suggestions concerning the fluctuations in Chester's continental trade during Elizabeth's reign.[1] According to this data the prosperity of the combined French and Spanish trades was at its greatest during the early years of Elizabeth's reign and for a short period during the 1580s before the outbreak of the Anglo-Spanish war. The earlier period of prosperity was based on a high level of iron imports and a more modest level of wine imports. After a sharp reduction during 1565–6 wine imports were maintained down to the early 1580s at roughly the level achieved in the early years of the reign, but iron imports declined steadily down to 1570 and then during the 1570s fluctuated at a level which was less than half the level achieved in the early period of prosperity. The annual average import of iron fell from about 260 tons for the five years between 1558–9 and 1565–6 to about 90 tons for the six years between 1583–4 and 1589.[2] The reduction in the volume of Spanish iron imported at Chester was in part replaced by the arrival of English iron; in 1585–6 and 1587–8 40 tons and 71 tons of English iron respectively were shipped to Chester.

The generally low level of trade during the late 1560s and 1570s can be explained by two phenomena. Firstly, the embargo on trade with Spain, which followed the seizure of Genoese treasure in 1568, must have had a dampening effect during the early part of this period, involving as it did a switch of normal trading channels, and secondly, the Chester merchants suffered severe losses during the 1570s due to the activity of pirates and through shipwreck. In about 1580 the Chester merchants claimed that since 1570 they had lost goods worth more than £12,000 by piracy; nine ships, two of which belonged to Chester, had been plundered. They also claimed that losses amounting to a further £10,500 had been sustained during shipwrecks along the coasts of France, Ireland and Wales and all of the ten ships involved belonged to Chester.[3]

The most disastrous single loss sustained by the Chester merchants occurred in 1575 when the *Bear Warwick* of Chester, a ship of 160 tons burthen, was attacked in the Irish Sea by five ships which had been fitted out in St. Malo. The loss, including the cargo of sack,

---

[1] See Appendix I (*a*) for details.

[2] Where the port books, customs accounts and local customs books give different details for the same year the higher total has been taken.

[3] P.R.O. S.P.D. 12/133/22, 15/27/89I.

spices and calico cloth, the money on board and the ship itself, was
estimated at £5,000. During the battle four men were killed and
another eleven were wounded.[1] Another incident worth relating
occurred four years later when the *Sunday* of Chester was plundered
twice within four months by Spanish pirates. The *Sunday* was sent
by its owner, William Ratcliffe of Chester, to Bilbao in March 1579
with a cargo of Manchester cottons and other goods worth about
£500. When the ship was within 40 leagues of Spain it was captured
by a man of war from Corunna and plundered of all its contents.
The crew and passengers were left without food by the pirates but
despite this reverse it was decided that the *Sunday* should proceed
with her voyage and collect a return cargo. This mission was eventually completed and the *Sunday* was returning from Spain, laden
with goods worth about £1,000, when she was attacked and plundered by two or three Spanish ships that were bound for Ireland.
During the resistance staged by the crew of the *Sunday* some of the
sailors were wounded and the Spaniards later hanged the *Sunday*'s
master.[2] It was incidents such as these that were helping to intensity
the cold war which existed between England and Spain for much of
Elizabeth's reign.

As can be seen from the incident involving the *Bear Warwick* it
was not only in continental waters that trouble from pirates was to
be expected. Piracy in the Irish Sea was widespread and perpetrated
by the English, Irish and Scots alike, as well as by the continentals,
and there is no doubt that piracy in this area was becoming increasingly serious during the 1560s and 1570s. In fact, quite close to
Chester in north Wales there were two important pirate centres
during Elizabeth's reign, at Beaumaris in Anglesey and Pwllheli in
Caernarvonshire.[3] One further example will suffice to demonstrate
the dangers due to piracy in the Irish Sea. It was reported in August
1581 that two pirate ships were lying in Beaumaris haven with 140
men and two prizes. These pirates plundered the *Margaret* of Hilbre
which was returning to Chester from Ireland. Unfortunately the
offenders were not captured but openly made sale of their cargo of
"ffyshe in divers partes alonge this Cooste to suche as came unto
(them) with Bootes and so departed".[4]

---

[1]Morris, p. 478; P.R.O. S.P.D. 15/27/89II.
[2]P.R.O. S.P.D. 12/150/55, 157/50.
[3]C. E. Hughes, 'Wales and Piracy, A Study in Tudor Administration 1500–1640,'
Unpublished M.A. Thesis (University of Wales, 1936), pp. 61, 267-8.
[4]P.R.O. S.P.Ireland 63/85/10, 86/61, 87/15; Chester R.O. M/L/5/30, 31. The
regularity of pirate activity in the Irish Sea can be seen by a quick glance at the
A.P.C. and S.P.

An interesting account of a shipwreck which occurred in 1567 has survived.[1] Again the ship was called the *Sunday* and William Ratcliffe, referred to as a mariner of West Kirby in the Wirral, was joint owner along with three Chester merchants, John Hewer, William Dodd and Thomas Tetlow. The *Sunday* was freighted by eight or more Chester merchants at Michaelmas 1567 for a voyage to Spain and the first half of the voyage was completed successfully. The ship was then laden with 36 tons of iron and 4 tuns of train oil for the return journey. The merchants who freighted the *Sunday* thought that the ship had needed repairing in Spain but claimed that this was not done. On the return journey the ship ran into bad weather near Waterford and was forced to ride at anchor. Eventually the ship's cables and anchor were found wanting and the ship had to be run ashore at which time "the merchauntes of the same (were) in greate daunger perill and losse of their lyves which by the grace of god were saved". The ship and some of the goods were lost and some of the rescued goods were later plundered by the local inhabitants so that only about a half of the cargo was eventually saved. The merchants who had freighted the *Sunday* tried to lay the whole blame on the owners who were referred to as "crafty and subtill persons" responsible for the accident because of their "necligence or defaulte". According to the ship's master and three of the sailors, however, the owners could not be blamed for what had happened. They claimed that the ship in fact had been repaired in Spain but unfortunately as they sailed close to England "they espyed a leake in the stemme before of the said bark". Had the wind been unfavourable they would have turned back for Spain but it was set fair for Chester so that "when wee saw the leake, our hartes were sore, but seinge the wynde was merye . . . we determyned to put all to god, and to beare homewardes".

It is doubtful whether the owners could be held responsible for these events. The *Sunday* was caught in a violent storm and the bowsprit and fore-sail were carried away following which the sailors cut away the main-mast to save the ship and tried to ride out the storm at anchor. Unfortunately "the fearsenes of the wynde and the storme beinge so great withall" the anchors and cables gave way and the ship ran aground.

Following the difficulties of the 1570s Chester's continental trade enjoyed a considerable boom during the last few years of peace. This boom was due entirely to a great increase in the import of

---

[1] P.R.O. Chester 2/229, mem. 4–5.

French wine; during the four years 1582–3 to 1585–6 annual wine imports averaged over 400 tuns compared with an annual average of about 145 tuns for six years in the 1570s. This sudden burst of activity was probably the result of the removal of wine duty at Chester in 1567;[1] an earlier boom in this trade being precluded by the difficulties of the 1570s.

From the scanty information available for the later 1580s it would seem that the war against Spain had a depressing effect on the import of both wine and iron at Chester. After this brief recession, however, these trades, and especially the wine trade, recovered to a remarkable extent during the 1590s; indeed the level of trade during the 1590s seems to have been at a rather higher level than during the difficult period of the 1570s. Clearly the expedients which were adopted to circumvent the official embargo on trade were beginning to pay dividends. The limited evidence at present available for other ports would suggest that after a rather lean time during the later 1580s Anglo-Spanish trade recovered somewhat during the last decade or so of the war.

Looking at the whole of the sixteenth century it is clear that Chester's period of greatest prosperity in the combined French and Spanish trades lies outside Elizabeth's reign. During the 1530s the importance of Chester as a centre of the wine and iron trades stood at its peak for the sixteenth century; in that decade more than 4,000 tons of Spanish iron and almost 3,000 tuns of wine were imported.[2] But despite the reduction in the volume of wine and iron imported during the 1540s and 1550s Chester was still handling more continental trade than at any time during the fourteenth and fifteenth centuries,[3] and it seems likely that the annual import of wine alone reached an all-time peak for the sixteenth century during the 1580s. There is no doubt that taken as a whole the sixteenth century was a time of prosperity for Chester compared with the fourteenth and fifteenth centuries.

After the golden decade of the 1530s Chester faced a series of difficulties which were not easily surmounted. In the last years of Henry VIII's reign the war against France and the increasing tension between England and Spain led to a reduction in Chester's trade with those countries. It has also been suggested that in the middle decades of the sixteenth century Chester began to experience

---

[1]See below pp. 77–8.
[2]Wilson II, p. 14.
[3]Wilson I, p. 138.

the competition of Liverpool for the first time in the continental trades.[1] As we have seen, this competition was maintained down to the outbreak of war in 1585. During Elizabeth's reign Chester's continental trade fluctuated between good times when the volume of trade began to approach the level of the 1530s and bad times when the volume of imports stood at less than half the level achieved in that decade.

II—*The trade with other areas of the continent*

Only a small amount of trade was conducted with countries north of France and imports from this area seem to have come exclusively from Scandinavia and the Baltic. One ship only is recorded as arriving at Chester from Norway; in October 1602 an Amsterdam ship reached Chester from Bergen with a cargo of 300 deal boards. A rather more regular trade existed between Chester and the Baltic.[2] In 1585–6 two cargoes were shipped to Chester from the Baltic. In October 1585 a Chester ship arrived from Elbing carrying 4½ lasts of flax, 16 lasts of tar and pitch, 50 "hundred tarred cable yarn",[3] 3 "danske"[4] chests and 16 pairs of playing tables. Ten months later, in August 1586, the *Maryan* of Rotterdam arrived at Chester from "Danske" carrying 400 quarters of "Danske rye" which was said to belong to a certain Robert Peacock. The customs account gives no more than this brief outline concerning the arrival of the cargo of rye at Chester but there is an interesting story connected with it which can be told from another source. At Easter 1586 the mayor of Chester and a number of leading citizens decided, because of the great dearth and scarcity of corn on the Chester market, to arrange for some rye to be brought into the city. To this end they dispatched Thomas Linial and David Lloyd, two of the city's merchants, to Hull where they made a bargain with Robert Peacock of Hull for a cargo of rye to be priced at 24*s.* the London quarter. The council meeting held on the 12 August decided that the rye should be taken up as a common bargain and

---

[1]*Ibid*, p. 137.

[2]In a recent article I suggested that trade between the Baltic and Chester was not established until the early seventeenth century. Woodward, 'The Chester Leather Industry', *op. cit.*, p. 86. This statement, which was based on the Chester port books (E190s), is clearly incorrect as is shown by the customs accounts (E122s) and local customs books (S.C.E.s) subsequently studied.

[3]Probably meaning 50 cwt.

[4]*i.e.* Danzig.

should not be thrown onto the market immediately but sold as the citizens needed it at "resonable prises".[1]

The city fathers were determined to relieve the scarcity at Chester during this year of high prices. In June and July 1586 they stopped a cargo of wheat, rye and peas from being shipped out of the Dee and ordered that it should be placed on the open market to relieve the scarcity.[2] Despite such efforts, however, the crisis continued and late in 1586 the council was once again exploring ways to relieve the scarcity in the city. A council meeting held on 24 November was told about the large quantity of grain that had arrived at Hull and promptly appointed David Lloyd and Richard Rathbone, another of the city's merchants, to ride over to Hull to secure some of this grain for the city.[3] The result of this journey is not recorded but it is reasonable to assume that Lloyd and Rathbone achieved success initially; in February 1588 the council was told of a suit which the city had before the Court of Common Pleas in the names of David Lloyd and Richard Rathbone against a certain Mr. Smith for a breach of contract and failure to deliver a bargain of "danske rye" to Chester.[4]

Towards the end of 1586 the city received more help in the struggle against starvation. At the council meeting held on 7 December there was a discussion about a cargo of 800 bushels of rye, Chester measure,[5] which had arrived from London. Of this the council secured 500 bushels for a common bargain but stipulated that members of the council should not have any part of the grain.[6] Further help came in the same month; on 3 December the *Gift of God* of London arrived at Chester from Ipswich carrying 340

---

[1]Chester R.O. A/B/1/f.203 r & v. The sale of the rye realized £753 6s. 4d. of which £717 15s. 9d. went to pay Robert Peacock and disburse other costs. The balance was to be used for the benefit of the city's poor. *Ibid*, f.204.

[2]Chester R.O. M/L/5/59–75. Both Burghley and Walsingham were kept informed of the progress of this operation.

[3]Chester R.O. A/B/1/f.207. Lloyd and Rathbone were given £10 to cover their expenses.

[4]*Ibid*, f.216.

[5]Chester had its own corn measure for most of Elizabeth's reign. The Chester bushel was about 26 gallons and 2½ Chester bushels were equal to one London quarter. P.R.O. S.P.Ireland 63/76/11; 81/22; 84/41. In 1602 a set of new measures were sent to Chester and the bushel was a standard bushel stamped with the Crown Imperial and the Exchequer stamp. Because of damage this bushel was replaced in 1614 and this new bushel is preserved at Chester. I am grateful to Mrs. E. Berry for providing me with this information.

[6]Chester R.O. A/B/1/f.208.

quarters of flour from Danzig.[1] It was, no doubt, because of the urgent need to secure additional supplies of grain during years of bad harvest that the city council, in March 1587, petitioned the Earl of Derby for "libertie to traffique to danske And other places in those contres".[2] Such a grant would be necessary if the Chester merchants were to trade directly with the Baltic for this trade was controlled by the Eastland Company, which had been established in 1579, to which they did not belong.

Interest in the Baltic trade was maintained during the later 1580s; in July 1587 the *Gods Gift* of London arrived at Chester carrying 400 quarters of rye, London measure, from Königsberg[3] which belonged to a London merchant and another 344 quarters of rye, London measure, probably shipped from Danzig originally, arrived from Ireland.[4] Three years later five Chester merchants brought a cargo from "Danske" which included 8 lasts of flax and 10 lasts of pitch and tar.[5]

Trade with the Baltic was probably not a new development of the 1580s; in April, May and September 1560 the "*Mearemade* de Flusshinge", the *Fawcon* of Dover and a Chester ship carried 380 quarters and 300 barrels of rye to Chester. Two of these ships also carried some soap, bottles, black paper, trenchers, pots, pitch and glasses, which suggests that they may have come from London or the Low Countries rather than direct from the Baltic. Two years later, in June 1562, one "Henry Kewderston easterling" imported 140 quarters of rye at Chester in two cargoes. This rye probably came from the Baltic although it is certain that one of the ships called in at an Irish port to pick up 800 sheepskins. Kewderston also imported three cargoes, comprising 330 quarters of rye, at Liverpool during the year 1562–3.[6]

---

[1] P.R.O. E190/1325/21. This is called a Liverpool port book but contains information about the trade of Chester.

[2] Chester R. O. A/B/1/f.208v.

[3] Referred to in the port book as "Quenborowe in Sprusland."

[4] P.R.O. E122/31/24. The entry for 18 July records that the *Jonas* of Chester, burthen 24 tons, arrived from Dublin with the rye and some caddows, timber and 4 "dansk" chests. One of the merchants involved was a certain William Atkyn. The Liverpool port book which contains entries for Chester (E190/1325/21) records that the *Jonas* of King's Lynn, burthen 60 tons, arrived from "Dannske" and its master was William Atkyn. No cargo was entered in the port book for this ship which may have trans-shipped its cargo to the Chester ship at some stage.

[5] Also 60 bowstaves, 8 dozen "cork for shoemakers", and 2 dozen glass bottles.

[6] P.R.O. E.122/31/5; 200/4.

The irregularity of the trade with the Baltic was due to two main factors. Firstly, the voyage to Chester was rather long and difficult and secondly, the main commodity of this trade, rye, was subject to a fluctuating demand which depended on the state of the harvest at home. Grain from the Baltic tended to arrive at Chester during years of bad harvest; that the harvests of 1560 and 1562 were bad[1] will help to explain the import of grain during the early 1560s. During the 1580s harvests were on the whole good but the harvest of 1585 was rather poor and the harvest of 1586 was bad;[2] as we have seen, Chester was short of grain during the mid 1580s and obtained additional supplies from the Baltic. The mid 1590s saw what were undoubtedly the worst harvests of Elizabeth's reign when "the rains fell incessantly all over Europe from Ireland to Silesia" and in Italy and Germany "poor people ate whatever was edible—fungi, cats, dogs, and even snakes".[3] Whether or not Chester obtained any relief from the Baltic is not recorded but the city fathers were anxious to supplement the supply of grain and avoid mass starvation. In July 1597 a Scottish merchant, named William Hunter, wrote to the mayor of Chester from Bristol offering to bring two or three ships to the Dee laden with malt and peas. The mayor wrote back immediately saying that although the prices seemed rather high the city was beholden to him for the offer and gave Hunter the liberty to sell his cargoes at Chester.[4] Early in the following year the mayor told the council that Thomas Offley of London, the prominent son of a Chester merchant, had agreed to send two ships full of corn to Chester on condition that the city paid for two "pylates".[5]

Thus the import of grain at Chester, particularly from the Baltic, tended to occur during years when the production of grain at home was deficient. Data provided by Professor Hoskins has been used to pinpoint years of poor harvests and this can be supplemented for Chester by comments made by William Aldersey, one of the leading Chester merchants who is referred to in Chapter 6 as the *second* William Aldersey, in a chronicle he compiled of significant events which occurred during his life. He recorded that 1562 was "a deare yeare of Corne, a buz (i.e. bushel) wheat at

---

[1] W. G. Hoskins, "Harvest Fluctuations and English Economic History, 1480–1619", *Agricultural History Review*, 12 (1964), p. 37.

[2] *Ibid*, pp. 37, 39.

[3] *Ibid*, p. 38.

[4] Chester R.O. M/MP/8/136, 137; M/L/5/146 r & v.

[5] Chester R.O. A/B/1/f.251.

17*s.*, Rye 15*s.*" while in 1585 "Corne (was) very deare . . . wheat at twentie shillinges the buz, Rye at fifteene, barley at twelve". Over the country as a whole the harvest of 1584 had been good but in the Chester region prices were high in 1585 because of a great storm which raged during the evening of 24 July 1584:

> "from noone untill midnight there was such thunder with lightning, haile and Raine continually without intermission that . . . haye and Corne (were) much destroyed by the haile and waters . . . and diverse men and Cattle with the lightbolt sleyne and hurte in diverse places".

In 1586, when the harvest was poor all over the country, things were even worse, "Corne grew marvelous deare, wheat at 26*s.* 8*d.* the buz, Rye 18s., the like not seene before". Then during the mid 1590s, in line with the national trend, prices increased still further. In 1595

> "Corne grew very deare rising from 12*s.* the buz. untill wheat came to 24*s.* and dearer and Rye after that Rate & price, and alsoe other victualls, likewise at a great price not onely here but generally through this land".

In 1596 prices increased still further to reach 28*s.* or more the bushel in January 1597 and 40*s.* the bushel in April.[1] It is significant that, during Elizabeth's reign, Aldersey referred to the price of grain only during these years of dearth when supplies on the Chester market were deficient and imports were necessary to maintain local standards of consumption.

Trade with countries north of France was almost entirely one way traffic; the port books and various customs accounts record only a single cargo that was shipped to this area. In July 1593 William Ratcliffe of London loaded 27 tons of lead ore, 4,000 rough horns and 5 cauldrons of coal aboard the *Thomas and John* of London to be sent to Flushing. John Bavand, one of the Chester merchants, made good his opportunity and placed 8 dickers of calfskins aboard the same ship. Apart from this there is no concrete evidence of any goods being shipped to markets north of France.[2]

---

[1] B. M. Additional MSS. 39925 fos. 20v, 21–22v. Aldersey used the Chester bushel as his standard of measurement (see p. 50) and the prices quoted are presumably maximum prices for a particular year rather than the annual average. Hoskins, *op. cit.*, pp. 37, 46.

[2] In April 1577 "Jacose Vandonstene" shipped 20,000 rough horns and 12 tons of coal from the Dee in the *Peter* of Hastings. Both the name of the merchant and the cargo suggest that the destination of the *Peter* may have been the Low Countries.

III—*Shipping and the continental trades*

Ships belonging to Chester were involved in the French and Spanish trades in most years, but the proportion of trade carried by Chester ships fell during Elizabeth's reign. The decline of Chester's ocean-going fleet was most evident towards the end of the period and most likely was due to the heavy loss of shipping suffered during the 1570s and the dangers to be faced from pirate and enemy vessels during the war. In most years the average burthen, or carrying capacity, of the Chester ships was about 40 tons although in 1565–6 the average burthen was only about 33 tons.[1] Some of the Chester ships engaged in this trade were quite small, such as the *Trinity White*, burthen 20 tons, which sailed for Galicia in July 1566 but others were much larger, such as the *Bear Warwick* of 160 tons or the *Hopewell* and *Peter*, of 80 and 100 tons respectively, that traded with France towards the end of the period.

The constant danger from pirates and privateers in the French and Spanish trades meant that merchant ships, especially when sailing alone, had to be well armed. Thus when one of the Chester ships was freighted out to some merchants in 1584 it was agreed that the ship should be well furnished with sufficient tackle, apparel, sails, powder and shot.[2] Ships could be protected further by sailing to and from the continent in pairs or convoys in the hope that a show of force would deter opposition. In some years ships tended to to leave, or arrive at, Chester on the same day probably to reduce the risk of piracy. Thus in March 1566 the *Trinity* and *Grace Jewett*, both of Chester and both bound for Spain, left Chester on the same day. The *Trinity* arrived back at Chester in July accompanied by the *Nicholas* of Douglas. Similarly the *William* and *Magdalene*, both of Chester, returned together at the end of May 1566. In the same way the *Sunday*, *Trinity* and *Katherine*, all of Chester, left for the continent together on 15 April 1577. These ships probably stayed together during the whole of their voyage for they returned to Chester with cargoes of iron in June. In 1582–3 little use was made of the convoy system in trading to and from Chester but in 1584–5, probably due to the increased tension between England and Spain, about half the ships sailing to and from Chester were accompanied

---

[1]See Appendix I(C). The tonnage figures given in the port books and quoted here only give a very approximate guide to a ship's size; the same ship is sometimes listed two or more times in the same port book, often being given a different burthen on each occasion.

[2]B. M. Harl MSS. 2091 f.271. After the capture of the *Bear Warwick* the ship and ordnance were valued at just over £1,200. Morris, p. 472.

by other ships. In the later years covered by the port books there was little tendency for the ships to go in convoy to and from Chester.

During the sixteenth century the government tried to encourage ships to sail in convoy. As early as 1552 the privy council ordered that ships should return from Spain in companies of not less than 10 or 12 at a time.[1] Twenty seven years later the privy council advised the Spanish Company in London and elsewhere, because of the danger from pirates and Turkish galleys, not to allow their ships "to goe into Spaine straglinge aparte" but to send them in convoy.[2] During the war with Spain the government took more active steps to ensure the safety of English merchant shipping. On 26 November 1591 a letter was sent from the privy council to all the head ports, including Chester, which said that ships should go to La Rochelle and Bordeaux for wines in the following year under convoy. It said that the convoy system had been used in the previous year, and although ships trading to the outports had taken advantage of it the whole cost of protecting the convoy had fallen on the London merchants. The cost of the convoy for 1591–2 was to be laid on all merchants at a rate of 3*s.* a tun on wine and all other goods.[3] The Chester merchants, however, were exempted from the convoy charges for 1591–2. This privilege was granted because of the extra distance that had to be travelled without the convoy by ships going to Chester, because a Chester ship had returned before the convoy had been formed, and because the privy council had been reminded about the losses sustained by the Chester merchants through shipwreck and piracy.[4]

In 1592–3 because additional trouble was expected from French men-of-war it was ordered that the convoy system should be continued. The Queen was to provide two ships to protect merchant shipping and a charge of 5*s.* a ton was to be levied on all goods except salt.[5] Chester was included in this new proposal. Burghley wrote to the customs officials who were responsible for collecting this levy, on 28 March 1593. He said that some "evil person" had intercepted the letter sent to Chester in November 1592 about the convoy and ordered the customs officials to draw up a list of persons bringing wine and other goods to Chester from France since

---

[1] J. A. Williamson, *Maritime Enterprise, 1485–1558* (Oxford, 1913), p. 225.
[2] *A.P.C.* XI, p. 137.
[3] *Ibid*, XXII, pp. 86–7.
[4] *Ibid*, p. 513.
[5] *Ibid*, XXIII, pp. 319–22.

November. Such merchants were to pay the 5s. levy, as in other
ports, and anyone refusing to do so was to be sent immediately
before the Queen.[1] In his reply to Burghley the mayor said that the
Chester merchants alleged that they were exempt from this levy.
The merchants said that they were given no aid by the convoy and
had therefore to man their ships with two or three times as many
men as usual, and yet they had still suffered some loss. Nevertheless
the mayor said that he was sending one or two merchants to London
to explain the case, and he finished by asking Burghley to be good
to the "poore merchauntes of this corporacon".[2] Whether or not
the Chester merchants did pay this levy in 1593 does not appear.
It seems likely, however, that the ships provided by the Queen and
the measures taken by the merchants themselves to defend their
ships were successful for the Chester merchants do not seem to have
suffered great losses through piracy or enemy action during the
1590s.

Elizabethan trade, when compared with the rush and bustle of
the present day, was a leisurely affair. Ships belonging to Chester
never made more than two return journeys to the continent in any
one year and a round voyage to the continent and back took
anything from two to six months. On any particular voyage the
Chester ships often traded with more than one port as in 1566
when the *Trinity* made a summer run to Spain leaving Chester in
March for Vigo and returning in July from Bermeo. In the same
year three ships left Chester for "Biscay" which suggests that they
were not bound for a particular destination but would trade where
the advantages seemed greatest. When a ship returned to Chester
there was no great rush to prepare it for another voyage. The
shortest period that a ship lay at Chester waiting to return to the
continent was about a month and some ships waited as long as four
months before making another trip. The tendency for voyages to
France or Spain to be protracted was due in part to the contrariness
of the weather or the need to wait for a convoy to form, but it was
also due to the need for careful salesmanship and the desire to seek
a good profit. A manual intended as a guide for merchants stressed
the necessity of a leisurely approach to trade:

> "And commonlye there can be nothinge well sold when you shalbe
> bounde to lade the same shipp backe againe within XXV or

---

[1] Chester R.O. M/L/1/33.

[2] Chester R.O. M/L/5/110. A list of wine and other commodities imported from
France in 1593 was drawn up. M/L/5/111.

thirttie dayes. Therefore, when you thincke to gaine, you lose. Therefore adverticement is good and the principall thinge that belongethe to A Merchaunte."[1].

The Chester ship which was shipwrecked on the coast of Ireland in 1567 had been in Spain for some five or six weeks "parte for ladinge, partly for wynde and wether".[2]

It is not possible to say how most of the voyages from Chester were organised but the copy of one charter party has survived which helps to throw some light on the matter. In 1584 Thomas Linial, one of the Chester merchants, contracted to hire the ship he owned to some unnamed merchants. Linial guaranteed that the ship was in good condition and agreed to appoint a master to the ship with fifteen sailors and a boy to help him. The merchants were authorised to load up to 60 tons of commodities on board and the ship was to sail to the Bay of Bilbao where it was to remain for two days until the merchants, or their factors, decided whether to unload at Bilbao, Bermeo or San Sebastian. No definite time during which the ship could remain in the chosen port was stipulated although both 28 and 30 days were crossed out. Finally for every ton of freight or for every "ton room" the merchants were to pay 42s. and it was agreed that the ship's boat should attend the merchants or their factors at all times during the voyage.[3]

Ships from other English and Welsh ports played an important part in Chester's overseas trade and on the whole they were larger than the Chester ships. The average size of such ships in 1582–3 was about 56 tons burthen while in later years covered by the port books the average was about 80 tons burthen. One of the largest ships to arrive at Chester was the *Hercules* of Rye, burthen 130 tons, which came from La Rochelle in 1603.[4]

IV—*Merchants in the continental trades*

Throughout Elizabeth's reign a large proportion of the trade with France and Spain was controlled by the Chester merchants. In most years they controlled over ninety per cent of the Manchester

---

[1]Tawney and Power, *op. cit.*, 3, pp. 207–8. "advertisement" probably means that the merchants should inform themselves of conditions in the local market rather than that they should inform others about their wares.

[2]P.R.O. Chester 2/229/mem.5.

[3]B. M. Harl MSS. 2091 f.271–7.

[4]Another large ship to arrive in that year was the *Hunter* of Enkhuizen, burthen 130 tons.

cottons and tanned calfskins shipped to the continent and seventy per cent or more of the iron and wine which arrived at Chester.

TABLE 13:

The Merchants in the French and Spanish Trades

(a) Exporting Manchester Cottons and Tanned Calfskins

	1562–3 %	1565–6 %	1576–7 %	1582–3 %	1584–5 %	1592–3 %	1602–3 %
Chester merchants	96·8	93·8	86·3	96·6	92·8	100·0	100·0
Other English Merchants	—	6·2	13·7	3·4	7·2	—	—
Foreign merchants	3·2	—	—	—	—	—	—

(b) Importing Wine and Iron

	1562–3 %	1565–6 %	1576–7 %	1582–3 %	1584–5 %	1592–3 %	1602–3 %
Chester merchants	77	95·5	95·5	74·6	70·0	97·7	96·3
Other English Merchants	—	4·5	4·5	25·4	16·5	—	3·7
Foreign merchants	23	—	—	—	13·5	2·3	—

The only merchant who did not live in Chester but traded through the city on a number of occasions was a certain Peter du Perry. He first appears in the customs accounts for 1562–3 which record that "Petro Pyrrye", alien, imported 56 tuns of Gascon wine. Two years later he was still importing wine through Chester; in January 1565 "peter perrin" shipped 50 tuns of wine and 5 tuns of vinegar to Chester. Perry does not reappear in the Chester customs accounts until the 1580s but in January and February 1573 "Peter du Pyrrye", described as a merchant lately of Bordeaux, shipped 300 goads of Manchester cottons, 1,500 tawed sheepskins and 40 quintals of copper "from the North" to Andalusia and a further 37 quintals of copper to St. Jean de Luz from Liverpool.[1] This copper was from the works of the Mines Royal Company in the Keswick area and it is interesting to note that an official of the company rode to Liverpool in 1572 about the debt of a certain "Peter du Perrei". Perry was arrested on account of this debt which he did not pay, although in May 1574 he sent £10 in part payment.[2]

During the early 1580s Peter du Perry, by then called a merchant of London, became the most important merchant in the Chester wine trade. He imported 88 tuns of wine, 29 tuns of wine and 74 tuns of wine in the years 1582–3, 1583–4 and 1584–5 respectively.

[1] P.R.O. E190/1324/4. Quintal—a 100 pounds or cwt.
[2] W. G. Collingwood, *Elizabethan Keswick, op. cit.*, p. 156.

Perry played a less important role in Chester's export trade; in 1582–3 he sent some leather and 600 goads of Manchester cottons to France while in 1584–5 he exported a further 3,000 goads of Manchester cottons to the continent. Apart from Perry no other English or continental merchant traded regularly with France and Spain through Chester although occasionally such merchants played an important role in the port's trade. English merchants who shipped the odd cargo to and from Chester came from London, Poole, Liverpool, Blackburn, Newcastle, Manchester and York.

During Elizabeth's reign the continental trade became concentrated in the hands of a smaller number of the city's merchants; in 1565–6 thirty one Chester merchants traded with France and Spain but the number had fallen to a mere fifteen by 1602–3.[1] This concentration of the trade in fewer hands was probably due in part to the losses sustained in the 1570s and also to the increased risks in the last two decades of Elizabeth's reign because of the war with Spain. It may also have been due partly to the restrictive policy pursued by a group of Chester merchants who joined the Spanish Company which was established in 1577.[2] Even at the beginning of Elizabeth's reign, however, the trade was dominated by a small group of merchants; in 1562–3, for example, eight merchants[3] controlled more than fifty per cent of the wine and iron which was shipped to Chester. By the end of the period the large merchants had tightened their grip on the city's trade; in 1602–3 another eight Chester merchants[4] controlled some eighty three per cent of the wine and sixty three per cent of the iron imported from the continent and ninety one per cent of the calfskins exported to France.

It is impossible to name all the Chester merchants who traded with the continent during Elizabeth's reign but a few can be picked out as being of special importance. Foulk Aldersey could be called the leading Elizabethan merchant mainly because of the length of his career. He became a freeman of the city in 1560–1[5] but did not begin to trade with the continent on his own account until 1565–6

---

[1] The number of merchants trading in other years were 21 in 1576–7, 25 in 1582–3, 18 in 1584–5 and 17 in 1592–3.

[2] See Chapter 5 for a discussion of this.

[3] Richard Strowbridge, Griffith Evans, Adam Goodman, Robert Evans, John Hewer, William Jewett, John White, John Middleton.

[4] Foulk, John, and two William Alderseys; Robert Berry, William Gamull, Edward Allen, William Johnson.

[5] *F.R.*, p. 36.

when he imported three tons of iron and shipped 600 goads of Manchester cottons to Spain. It seems likely that he filled in the intervening years by acting as an overseas factor for other Chester merchants. By 1576–7, however, Aldersey had emerged as the most important of the Chester merchants trading with the continent when he shipped 39 tons of iron to Chester and 1,900 goads of Manchester cottons and 34 northern straights to the continent. He continued to trade with the continent throughout Elizabeth's reign, and was always among the most important group of merchants. Adam Goodman and William Jewett were among the most important merchants in the early part of the period and William Massey, who began his trading career during the early 1560s, became one of the most important merchants in the middle decades of the reign along with others such as David Lloyd, David Mountford, Richard Knee, Thomas Tetlow, William Aldersey and Richard Bavand.[1]

At Chester, as in other places, it was customary to allow a widow to follow the occupation of her late husband until she married again. Thus Alice Massey, the widow of William Massey, imported 19 tons of iron from France in August 1593. William Massey must have died a little time before this because in March of that year he signed the port book himself. Letters written in 1594 and 1598 concerning the right of Alice Massey to continue as a merchant prove that she established herself as a regular merchant in the French trade during the following years.[2] She continued to trade with France until her death in the early seventeenth century for early in 1601 Gerard Massey, as executor of the will of Alice Massey, imported $4\frac{1}{2}$ tuns of wine through his factor Peter Newall. No other widow established herself regularly in the continental trade during Elizabeth's reign although occasionally a widow might be responsible for importing the odd cargo when administering her late husband's estate.

A few of the Chester merchants extended their business activities by trading through other ports in the north west and especially through Liverpool. In some years they controlled nearly a third of the iron shipped to Liverpool and controlled as much as two thirds of the Manchester cottons exported through that port.

---

[1] For details of the three William Alderseys trading with the continent during Elizabeth's reign see Chapter 6. There were two Richard Bavands—the elder who became a freeman of the city in 1557–8 and was mayor in 1581–2 and 1601 and the younger who became a freeman in 1581–2 *F.R.*, pp. 33, 55, 56, 84.

[2] Chester R.O. M/L/5/120–2, M/L/1/144, A/B/1/f.242.

TABLE 14:

Merchants in the Continental Trade of Liverpool[1]

(a) Exporting Manchester Cottons (in goads)

	1565–6	1569–70	1572–3	1573–4	1575–6	1579–80	1582–3	1584–5
Liverpool merchants	5,250	20,900	1,800	800	5,500	3,500	5,250	8,550
Chester merchants	1,450(21)	—	2,400(27)	1,800(69)	100(2)	300(8)	2,600(33)	700(7)
Other merchants	—	—	4,500	—	—	—	—	—
Total	6,700	20,900	8,700	2,600	5,600	3,800	7,850	9,250

(b) Importing Iron (in tons)

	1565–6	1569–70	1572–3	1573–4	1575–6	1579–80	1582–3	1584–5
Liverpool merchants	65½	61½	46½	50	15½	69½	101	92
Chester merchants	24½(26)	3 (1)	—	—	2 (9)	8 (10)	49(32)	31½(25)
Other merchants	4	114	13	—	5	—	—	—
Total	94	178½	59½	50	22½	77½	150	123½

[1]P.R.O. E190/1323/4, 9, 12; 1324/4, 6, 9, 22; 1325/9, 17. The figure in brackets is the approximate percentage of the trade controlled by the Chester merchants.

Chester merchants exerted most control over Liverpool's trade
in 1582–3 when Richard Knee, Foulk Aldersey, David Lloyd and
Richard Holker controlled about 33 per cent of the Manchester
cottons exported and about 32 per cent of the iron imported. In
addition Roger Hanmer imported 10 tuns of French wine out of a
total of 38 tuns imported in that year. The Chester merchants also
traded through Beaumaris on occasion; in 1562–3 William Jewett
imported 78 tuns of sack and 40 tons of Spanish iron through
Beaumaris while another three Chester merchants imported a
further 15 tuns of sack.[1]

The smuggling of prohibited commodities helped to extend
further the business activities of the Chester merchants. A number
of the merchants were exporting tanned calfskins to the continent
before 1584, that is, before they were legally entitled to do so.[2]
During or shortly after 1581 the privy council set up a commission
to inquire into the alleged export of tanned calfskins from Chester.[3]
The commission took evidence from twenty-two people, most of
whom were directly involved in the smuggling of calfskins, and it
appears that in the year beginning March 1581 quantities of
leather and calfskins had been exported to France and Spain in
five vessels. Twelve of the Chester merchants including Richard
Bavand, Foulk Aldersey, Richard Knee, William Massey, Thomas
Tetlow and David Mountford were named by various witnesses as
being involved. David Mountford, himself accused of smuggling,
had the audacity to claim that many of his fellow merchants were
"Culpable in Carring and conveying over of Calveskynnes and
leather". Detailed examination of the witnesses revealed two instances when the smugglers used violence against the customs
officials. On one occasion two of the officials apprehended the smugglers loading a lighter with calfskins during the night ready to
be carried down-stream to an ocean-going vessel waiting at Neston
but they were prevented from seizing the cargo by some of the
merchants and their accomplices. Richard Knee played a leading
role in this affair. It was claimed that he "dyd plucke the sayd
Fowlke (Foulk Edwards one of the officials) backe by the garment"
and the other customs official, Piers Middleton, said that

> "with greate violence and stronge hand the sayd knee dyd take
> the staff of this deponent by thende and this deponent in his

---

[1]P.R.O. E122/31/5; 200/4.
[2]Leather could be exported only under special licence.
[3]P.R.O. E178/7224, 7220, 498.

owne defence, drewe a lytle dagger that he had and with that the same knee drewe his dagger affirming with many greate othes if this examinant would not . . ."

Unfortunately the manuscript is damaged at this point and what Knee threatened to do to Middleton must remain a mystery. Among Knee's "ayders and asisters" was Foulk Aldersey armed with a short bill, the point of which he held towards the body of Foulk Edwards. On another occasion a customs officer was deterred by gunfire from searching a ship which was suspected of carrying a cargo of leather. Perhaps the most revealing statement in the whole affair came from the master of a Plymouth ship who said that the Chester merchants "do comonly use to sende there merchandyces to the shippes by night".

This type of incident was not unusual during Elizabeth's reign. During the mayoralty of Sir John Savage, 1574–5, a customs officer, also investigating the smuggling of leather, was attacked by a mob at Chester.[1] About eight years later at Liverpool a young customs officer who attempted to seize a cargo of leather was attacked and wounded by a group of merchants who appear to have been led by Gyles Brookes, one of the most prominent Liverpool merchants. Eleven months after this first incident Brookes had another meeting with the same officer, a certain Simon Tetlow aged about nineteen. On this occasion Brookes and five other men assaulted Tetlow; Brookes, incensed by Tetlow's continued inquisitiveness, said that "yf he found him ther another night he would cutt of his yeares".[2]

During Elizabeth's reign many members of the Chester merchant community were visitors to the continent. In February 1562 an unnamed Chester merchant arrived at Bilbao having travelled overland from Seville and a few months later another Chester merchant was ready to sail from Bilbao with letters from Sir Thomas Challoner, the English ambassador to Spain.[3] Another Chester merchant, William Pillen, was in Lisbon during 1578 and on his return to England informed the privy council about the activities of Sir Thomas Stukeley, the English renegade, with whom he had dined. Pillen had first seen Stukeley about ten years earlier at Vigo in Spain.[4] Similarly Brian Bland, who was described as one

[1]B. M. Harl MSS. 1996 f.3.
[2]P.R.O. E178/499.
[3]*Cal. S.P. Foreign*, 1561–2, pp. 540–1; 1562, pp. 228–9.
[4]*Cal. S.P.D. Eliz.*, Addenda 1566–79, pp. 542–3.

of the merchants detained in Spain by the King's restraint, arrived back in Chester in 1586. He was sent to London to be interviewed by Burghley who, it was thought, would be able to obtain from him "many good notes of the Spanish intencions".[1] In the same year it was feared that Richard Holker of Chester was dead at St. Jean de Luz and in the Armada year the Chester council was informed that William Browne, who was a council member, had died in Spain.[2] Exactly what these Chester citizens were doing on the continent is not clear. No doubt some were attending to their own business but others were probably acting as factors for other Chester merchants. None of the men mentioned above were among the more prominent merchants which would suggest that at least a part of their time was spent acting as factor for other merchants.

Some details are available concerning the activities of William Coitmore who had served his apprenticeship under Foulk Aldersey and died in France in the early seventeenth century.[3] Coitmore's trading activities during the winter of 1600–1 can be recreated from the port book for that period. On 24 October 1600 he signed the port book as Foulk Aldersey's factor. Following this he probably went to France for on 12 January 1601 he entered, in the port book, details of goods brought from France in the names of himself, Foulk and William Aldersey. He probably returned to France in February for on the 6th of that month he entered the details of goods belonging to Foulk Aldersey and himself that were being shipped to France. Coitmore was still in France two months later when he entered into a bond with William Aldersey, to whom he owed 25 French crowns, which ended "in witness hereof I sett hereunto my hand in Bordexe this 17th of Aprill 1601 per me Willm Coytmor". Coitmore eventually died in France and one of the William Alderseys, probably the third William Aldersey who died in 1625,[4] was accused of wrongly administering his goods. In reply to one accusation Aldersey said that he had disposed of two of Coitmore's cheeses amongst the merchants as was usual in such cases in a "stranger Cuntrie being but trifles". In a later statement he referred to the "marchantes of Chester for whome Coytmore

[1]P.R.O. S.P. Ireland 63/125/1. When Bland became a Chester freeman in 1574 he was described as a mariner. *F.R.*, p. 47.

[2]Chester R.O. A/B/1/fos. 201, 217.

[3]*F.R.*, p. 76. Cheshire R.O. W.C. 1602–3 William Coitmore. He became a freeman of Chester in 1596.

[4]See below pp. 106–9.

was putt in truste as factor".[1] Unfortunately there is no more information concerning either the role of the factor in the French and Spanish trades or the rewards that could be made from acting as a factor for the merchants of a small outport.

It is clear, however, that the Chester merchants did not rely entirely on the services of factors sent over to France and Spain but placed some of their business interests in the hands of continental merchants. When John Aldersey died in 1605 he bequeathed to his son William, among other things, "all my goods which are due to me in Mr. Dumas his handes in Bourdeaux".[2] Detail of another business transaction has survived but this time it is not clear whether or not the foreign merchant was actually working for his Chester counterparts. Early in Elizabeth's reign four Chester merchants made an agreement with Peter du Perry, described as a merchant of Bordeaux. It seems that the Chester merchants had broken their part of the bargain so that Perry stood to lose not only his wines but a further £500 also. The privy council referred this case to William Glaseour, the vice-chamberlain of Chester, who was to see that Perry should have "no furder juste cawse of complainte".[3]

---

[1] Cheshire R.O. W.C. 1602–3 William Coitmore.
[2] Cheshire R.O. W.S.1605 John Aldersey. See also W.C. 1606 John Aldersey, where reference is made to the calfskins in the hands of "John dumas in Bordeaux."
[3] *A.P.C.* VII, pp. 332–3.

4

THE COASTING AND INLAND TRADES

"It Served north walles Lancashire Coventrye, and the Countres
adioyninge, with wines Irone woade fyshe etc. Where now since
the Spoylles, and losse of the wholle navie, These places are
growne in trade with Lonndone & Bristowe, and receve theire
Commodities thence, to the ruyne of the Citie".
(Petition of about 1580 concerning the decayed state of Chester.)[1]

I—*The coasting trade*

CHESTER played an important role in the north-western region[2]
by supplying a wide range of commodities to the smaller
ports and coastal towns and receiving in return a smaller
range of commodities produced, for the most part, in the hinterlands of these places. In addition the coasting trade brought
commodities to Chester from further afield and especially from
London.

The volume of coasting traffic passing through Chester fluctuated
considerably during the period and to a large extent the fluctuations
were caused by changes in the volume of grain and pulse shipped
from the Dee which was destined especially for the ports of north
west Wales and, to a smaller extent, for the ports of Lancashire,
Cumberland and Westmorland.

TABLE 15:

The Number of Ships Involved in the Coasting Trade[3]

	1576–7	1582–3	1584–5	1586–7	1592–3	1595 (6 months)	1598 (6 months)	1602–3
To Chester	4	—	1	7	25	6	9	22
From Chester	6	18	10	7	29	23	9	66

[1]P.R.O. S.P.D. 12/158/4.

[2]Interpreted loosely to include north-west Wales.

[3]For references see Appendix III (i).

TABLE 16:

The Shipment of Grain and Pulse from the Dee
(to the nearest quarter)[1]

	1576–7	1582–3	1584–5	1586–7	1592–3	1595 (6 months)	1598 (6 months)	1602–3
Wheat	41	72	95	—	232	—	18	264
Barley	62	206	90	—	216	—	—	935
Malt	60	9	72	—	100	—	—	185
Oats	—	54	—	—	—	—	40	600
Rye	—	—	—	—	61	—	—	3
Peas	8	232	68	—	14	—	4	166
Beans	—	2	—	—	—	—	4	60
Peas and Beans	—	24	8	—	—	—	—	14
Total	171	600	333	0	623	0	66	2,227

Apart from this trade in basic foodstuffs the export sector of Chester's coasting trade closely resembled the Irish trade. A wide selection of commodities was shipped to other towns in the region ranging from the figs, raisins, oranges and lemons produced on the continent to the nails, wool cards and pieces of furniture made in England. It has been suggested that "Chester was the shopping centre which catered for the personal, household and occupation requirements of the inhabitants of Anglesey and Carnarvon".[2] This is amply borne out by the Chester port books. Beaumaris was by far the most important town within the whole region with which Chester traded; in fact this trade resembles, in miniature, the trade between Chester and Dublin. In the three years 1593–4, 1595–6 and 1599–1600 cargoes shipped to Beaumaris included 2,400 yards of canvas, 3,750 yards of linen cloth, 33¾ tons of iron, 15½ tuns of wine, more than 52 tons of salt and large quantities of other commodities including hops, alum, soap, madder and lead.[3] The trade with Beaumaris and other towns in the region provided Chester with a valuable outlet for goods shipped to the city from Ireland and the continent, and for goods carried overland from London and other places.[4]

[1]Quantities converted to the London measure. See above p. 50 for a discussion of the Chester measures.

[2]E. A. Lewis, *The Welsh Port Books, op. cit.*, p. xxxvii.

[3]*Ibid*, p. 263 et seq. for details of the large and varied cargoes shipped to Beaumaris. See also Appendix I(E) for details of the towns with which Chester traded.

[4]A peak in the shipment of wine and iron occurred in the summer six months of 1595 when over 11 tons of iron and 35¼ tuns of wine were carried to neighbouring Welsh and English towns.

The nature of the import sector of Chester's coasting trade tended to differ from year to year. In 1592–3 the trade was dominated by the import of Irish commodities from Liverpool while in the summer of 1595 the bulk of the imports comprised grain from the smaller ports of Lancashire.[1] At the very end of Elizabeth's reign this sector of trade was dominated by the import of considerable quantities of fish from the ports of south west England.

The most important feature in the import sector of the coasting trade was the regular arrival of large and miscellaneous cargoes from London. In most years, for which details of the coasting trade have survived, at least one ship arrived at Chester from London. Scores of different commodities were carried by the ships ranging from scales to sugar, from arrows to anvils, from "mylne stones" to madder, from paper to prunes and from tar to tin. But by far the most important commodities shipped to Chester were wine, chalk, fuller's earth and iron, described as Spanish or "Inglyshe"; twenty cargoes shipped to Chester between 1569 and 1603 contained a total of 49¾ tuns of wine, 65 tons of chalk, 143 tons of fuller's earth and 250½ tons of iron. The great majority of the cargoes arriving at Chester from London was controlled by Cestrians and the most prominent of these was Richard Bavand, a merchant and ironmonger,[2] who led the campaign against the attempt of the Spanish Company to control the trade of Chester during the late 1570s and 1580s.[3] He owned eight, and was part owner of another four, of the twenty cargoes shipped from London. Other prominent Chester merchants in this trade were Roger Lea, an ironmonger and owner of two cargoes, William Wall, an ironmonger and part owner of two cargoes, and Thomas Linial, a mercer by trade and owner of two cargoes and part owner of a third.[4]

The arrival of ships from London played an important part in the economic life of Elizabethan Chester. Supplementary supplies of some commodities that were normally imported direct from the

---

[1] It is interesting to note that grain was not shipped from Chester along the coast during this summer. In fact 1595 was a year of bad harvest when, presumably, the Chester citizens again found themselves short of food. Years when large quantities of grain were shipped from the Dee (viz. 1582–3, 1592–3 and 1602–3) all followed good harvests (viz. those of 1582 and 1583, 1592 and 1593 and 1602 and 1603). W. G. Hoskins, 'Harvest Fluctuations', *op. cit.*, pp. 37–39. In years of bad harvests the inhabitants of the Welsh coastal towns must have been very short of food.

F.R., pp. 33, 46, 56, 69.

[3] See chapter 5 for details of the campaign.

For details of their trades see *F.R.*, pp. 33, 35.

continent were obtained from this source as were some very bulky commodities, such as fuller's earth and chalk, which would have been very expensive and difficult to move overland. In addition a wide variety of less bulky commodities were shipped to Chester, some no doubt destined to be consumed in Chester and her hinterland, some no doubt destined to be shipped to Ireland or along the coast to Wales or towns north of Chester. Important as this trade with London was, however, it accounted for only a small proportion of the goods which were shipped from Chester to Ireland. To take just one example, only very small quantities of hops, one of the most important of Chester's exports to Ireland, arrived by sea from London, and many other commodities which never featured in the cargoes carried from London were exported to Ireland.

II—*The inland trade*

There is no doubt that Chester was heavily dependent on overland trading routes both for the distribution of commodities brought from overseas and for the collection of commodities to be shipped abroad. It was not only light luxury goods, such as the small quantities of fine fabrics exported to Ireland, that were carried overland but also bulky commodities such as hops. In 1580 a letter to Burghley stated that

> "All the Chapmen of this Cyttie do make there provysion of hoppes at london to furnishe there shopps with all . . . the Carryers of Chester Come Wekely to bosomes Inne in St Lorance lane, where Carraige may be had to this Cyttie; As I do remember for $\frac{3}{4}d$ the pounde, or at the uttermost A penny the pounde".[1]

In January 1581, Chester hop sellers demanding 4s. 6d. per cwt., that is 9s. a horse-load, for carriage from London. It was stated that wains would carry 2 cwt. for 8s. but, unfortunately, they "travell not nowe in Wynter".[2] Supplies for the troops in Ireland were often carried overland from London to Chester rather than being shipped direct to Ireland. In October 1585 the mayor of Chester wrote to the Earl of Derby about the provision of powder

[1]P.R.O. S.P. Ireland 63/78/51. According to N. Riches, *The Agricultural Revolution in Norfolk* (Chapel Hill, 1937), pp. 28–9 *Blossoms Inn* in Lawrence Lane was used as a carting centre in the eighteenth century.

It will be remembered that Robert Cutt, who lived in St. Lawrence Lane, was referred to as the "purveior of the Hoppes" who was "dailie acquainted with the Carriages that come hither." S.P. Ireland 63/83/33, 55. See above p. 32.

[2]P.R.O. S.P. Ireland 63/80/37.

for the army in Ireland but asked to be allowed to delay before fetching it to Chester because of the "depnes of the waies and the danger of Caryadge by waine from London".[1] Ten years later nineteen carts were detailed to carry powder, match and arms to Chester from London and sixteen days were allowed for the journey. The provision of nineteen spare axle-trees and a wheelwright to make running repairs by the road-side further indicates the state of sixteenth century roads.[2]

Although the evidence is rather thin it is clear that the carriers took some goods with them on the return journey to London. In 1566, for example, a pack of fells and a fardel of skins were carried to London, the latter being taken by "John Scons caryer".[3] John Sconce was a Chester citizen and when he died in 1585 his estate was valued at £28 16s. 8d which included two cows valued at £3 6s. 8d. It is clear that Sconce carried goods by pack-horse rather than by cart; his three horses and a mare were valued at £4, while his four pack-saddles and girths were valued at 10s.[4] Sometime later it was recorded that six bundles of cloth and skins "all had (gone) up to London" and similar commodities were said to have "gon to London" on other occasions.[5]

The Sheriff's Customs Books also give some evidence concerning the movement of other commodities from the city. The bulk of the linen yarn imported from Ireland was said to have "gon" and some, more specifically, was said to have "gon to Manchester". There are also recorded many instances of other commodities which had "gon" out of the city but in most cases no destination is given. Occasionally we are given more information and are told that 20 barrels of herrings had "gon to Wrexhm unsold" or that some figs had been carried to Manchester,[6] but usually the remark "gon" or "discharged hens" was considered sufficient.

---

[1]Chester R.O. M/L/1/19, M/MP/4/14.

[2]P.R.O. S.P. Ireland 63/178/95 March, 1595.

[3]Chester R.O. S.C.E., 11, 1565–6.

[4]Cheshire R.O. W.S. 33/35. Sconce also possessed five loads of hay valued at £2; there is no mention of the inventory of a cart. Another carrier, also called John Sconce, died in 1606 although he seems to have retired from business; his estate valued at £45 10s. comprised only household goods. W.S. 1606 John Sconce. These two men were probably not trained as carriers, "John Scons, baker" became a freeman in 1533 and "John Scons, cowper" became a freeman in 1585. *F.R.*, pp. 20, 60.

[5]Chester R.O. S.C.E., 12, 1571; for other examples see *ibid.*, 1578, 1579, 1580.

[6]*Ibid.*, 1578, 1580.

Other evidence concerning the distribution of commodities from Chester can be obtained from two household account books. The Shuttleworths of Gawthorpe Hall and Smithhills in Lancashire[1] frequently made purchases in Chester.[2] For example, in June, 1586, 18 "gallones of sake (and) towe hoggeshedd of wyne, whyte and clered" costing £8 5s., "halffe a tune of Spenishe ierone containge XXVth bares" costing £7 14s. 4d and some pitch were bought at Chester and carried to Smithhills at a cost of 17s.[3] Similarly during the next few years quantities of sack, cloth, silk, spices, soap, hair powder, wine and iron were purchased at Chester by the Shuttleworths.[4] Chester, however, was not the only market to serve the Shuttleworths; they also bought wine and iron at Liverpool, wine at Manchester, and spices and other commodities at London.[5] Wine also seems to have been bought at Chester for the household at Hornby Castle some eight and a half miles north of Lancaster. In 1582 a servant was paid 9s. 6d. for "riding from Hornby to Westchester (i.e. Chester) and Liverpool to see and buy wine for the Lord's use and to speak with the Lord's tenants".[6]

Few details have survived relating to the overland carriage of goods to and from Chester but it is possible to give a rough outline of this trade. The bulk of commodities exported through Chester probably arrived at the city overland. Regular journeys by the Chester carriers brought commodities from London and no doubt picked up consignments *en route*. In addition many English manufactured goods must have been carried to Chester overland— knives and other blade instruments from the Sheffield region, nails and other hardware perhaps coming from the Midlands, salt from Cheshire, cloth from Lancashire, Yorkshire, Wales, Westmorland and other areas. There is little evidence to support this but a large volume of commercial traffic was carried by many roads during the sixteenth century; that northern clothiers were prepared to send their cloths overland to London is well known and

---

[1]Gawthorpe Hall is about a mile and a half from Burnley; Smithhills is in Bolton county borough.

[2]"The House and Farm Accounts of the Shuttleworths of Gawthorpe Hall", (ed.) J. Harland, *Chetham Society Publications*, 35, 41, 43 (1856 & 1857).

[3]*Ibid.*, 35, p. 29.

[4]*Ibid.*, pp. 45, 59, 65, 67, 75, 78, 88. in 1590, ¾ of a ton of iron cost £10 13s. 8d.

[5]*Ibid.*, pp. 18, 80–1, 89, 106, 115.

[6]"A Sixteenth-Century Survey and Year's Account of the Estates of Hornby Castle Lancashire", (ed.) W. H. Chippindall, *Chetham Society Publications*, New Series, 102 (1939), p. 115. Wine was bought on a later occasion at Liverpool and Preston, *ibid*, p. 119.

from the late fifteenth century or early sixteenth century cloth was carried from Westmorland to Southampton by the pack-horse trains of Kendal.[1]

Chester was also an important distributive centre during the early modern period. Along with Liverpool it played an important role in supplying linen yarn and, to a lesser extent, wool for the developing textile industries of the north west. Other imports such as wine and iron were sent along the Lancashire and Welsh coasts and inland into Lancashire, Cheshire and other neighbouring counties.[2] It is impossible to define with any accuracy the extent of Chester's hinterland during this period but the citizens of Chester could not have consumed more than a small part of the commodities imported from overseas.

Overland carriage, especially of bulky commodities, was often slow and sometimes dangerous but sea-borne trade was none too safe during the sixteenth century. Dangers from piracy, the possibility of shipwreck and delays due to adverse weather conditions all reduced the advantages of shipping goods along the coast and the long sea route around the dangerous western coasts of England and Wales made the sea journey from London, and from other southern and eastern ports, to Chester particularly hazardous. These conditions, plus the small size of many of the vessels operating in the coasting trade, meant that the advantage to be gained by carrying goods along the coast rather than by road was less than is often imagined. In the trade between London and the hinterlands of ports such as Hull and Newcastle carriage by sea, especially of bulky commodities, always tended to be economically more viable than overland carriage but in the trade between London and Chester the land route, which was much shorter than the sea route, had much to recommend it.[3]

---

[1] B. C. Jones, "Westmorland Pack-Horse Men in Southampton", *Transactions of the Cumberland and Westmorland Antiquarian and Archaeological Society*, N.S., 59 (1960), pp. 65–84. The pack-horse men carried a wide variety of commodities back from Southampton. Other pack-horse men to visit Southampton came from Manchester, Yorkshire, Blackburn, Bolton and Nottingham.

[2] See the bond between Richard Spencer, a Congleton vintner, and Foulk Aldersey dated August, 1608. Spencer owed £10 10s. presumably for wine supplied by Aldersey. Cheshire R.O. W.S. 1609 Foulk Aldersey.

[3] The sea route from London to Chester was rather more than four times the length of the shortest overland route. If sea carriage in England was always more economical and convenient than land carriage supplies for the Mines Royal Company in the Keswick area would have been shipped from London to one of the Cumberland ports instead of to Newcastle and thence to Keswick via Barnard Castle and Stainmore. W. G. Collingwood, *Elizabethan Keswick, op. cit.*, pp. 78–9, 93, 104.

5

MERCHANT POLITICS

"the Elizabethans were incorrigible liars".[1]

THE merchant group in Elizabethan Chester was not a clearly defined body with a common purpose. At times the great majority of the merchants who traded with the continent combined together in opposition to other groups within the city but at other times they split into warring factions each seeking its own ends and attempting to overthrow the schemes of rival parties. On occasion, however, the whole city, including the merchant community, combined to present a united front in an attempt to secure some particular privilege.

Some aspects of the Gild Merchant survived at Chester throughout the sixteenth century and this body consisted of all the freemen of the city. During the reign of Mary, however, a new merchant company, distinct from this medieval survival, was incorporated. The new company, established in May 1554, was to consist of merchants who traded with the continent and no member was to be allowed to practise a manual occupation or sell by retail. It was to be governed by a master and two wardens and it received privileges similar to those granted to most trading companies; the right to make statutes and ordinances for governing its members, the privilege of perpetual succession, a common seal, the right to hold lands and tenements, and the right to sue and be sued in the law courts.[2]

Opposition to the new company, headed by the mayor, sprang up almost immediately. The mayor wrote to two of the city's aldermen, who were in London, to inform them of the situation and ask them to put the case before the Lord Chancellor.[3] One of the objections to the new company was that it contravened the constitutional organisation of the city in that the merchants refused to obey the mayor and city councillors but rather met together in "previe councells" to make ordinances to the derogation of the

---

[1]T. S. Willan, *Studies in Elizabethan Trade, op. cit.*, p. 160.

[2]C. Gross, *The Gild Merchant* (Oxford, 1890), 2, pp. 360–2; *Calendar of Patent Rolls, Philip and Mary, 1553–4*, p. 322; Morris, pp. 463–4.

[3]Chester R.O. M/L/5/265, November 1554.

ancient grants and charters of the city. The merchants were also said to compel those admitted to the company to "swere upon thevangelist" to keep their secrets. More weighty objections against the company were on economic grounds. It was alleged that previously all freemen of the city had been allowed to trade overseas but that this was prohibited by the company, who laid down a seven year apprenticeship as the necessary training for anyone who wished to become a merchant. The merchants were accused further of forcing craftsmen and tradesmen to sell their wares to them and not to merchant strangers. The way the merchants organised their business also antagonised the opposition; it was alleged that the great and rich merchants did "lymytte, Assigne and appoynt the yonge merchauntes what quantitie of wares he shall occupie and to what place the shipe shall go against the mynde of the owners of the said shipe" whereas previously any man could ship any amount of goods to whatever place he pleased. Another complaint was that the merchants were fixing prices so that the prices of "Irne, trayne, wode, flax, wyne & suche other are lately Inhauncede & Rysen fare above the olde prices". It was also feared that the rich merchants were withholding goods from the market hoping to raise prices, and there was some doubt as to whether the system of common bargains was to be continued.[1]

These objections were set down in a petition to the Lord Chancellor and, to stress the urgency of the case, it was claimed that the mayor and councillors were in great fear of public disorders and that unless the charter were speedily rescinded the city would be utterly ruined and would not be able to serve the Crown in its weighty affairs as always had been the custom.[2] Despite this voluble opposition the charter was not revoked, the city was not ruined, and, in the early part of her reign, Elizabeth saw fit to renew the charter.[3]

Although they were frequently referred to as merchant "venturers" or "adventurers" the Chester merchants had no organic connection with the national Merchant Adventurers' Company. There were branches of this company at York, Hull, Newcastle

---

[1]Chester R.O. M/L/5/266. No date, probably 1554. See also M/L/5/267 for a rough draft of a part of these objections to the company.

[2]Chester R.O. M/L/5/268. Undated, probably late 1554 or early 1555.

[3]B. M. Harl MSS. 2054 fos. 49–50, May 1559.

and other places[1] but not at Chester. In fact it was stipulated in the charter of 1554, and renewal of 1559, that the Chester merchants were not to interfere with the franchises of the Merchant Adventurers' Company.[2]

Two manuscripts have survived which list the members of the Chester merchant company.[3] In the first manuscript the names of forty three members are given while the second lists fifty three "marchuntes that be sworne of the Companye". Not all the members had been trained as merchants; both lists contain a number of drapers, a few ironmongers and tanners, a tailor and a mariner.[4] There seems little doubt that all those who traded with the continent were members of the company but it is also clear that not all members were actively engaged in trade. Indeed, as we have seen, there were fewer merchants trading with France and Spain than there were members of the company.

I—Co-operation

By the early years of Elizabeth's reign the friction between the city authorities and the merchant company had been reduced to the extent that the two parties could work together in a common cause. This cause resulted from the rationalisation of the customs system whereby Chester lost her old status as a palatinate port and was brought into the national customs system.[5] In June 1558 William Glaseour, a vice-chamberlain of the palatinate, was appointed collector of customs, subsidies, tonnage and poundage at Chester and ordered to submit his accounts to the royal exchequer in London.[6]

---

[1]W. E. Lingelbach, *The Internal Organisation of the Merchant Adventurers of England* (Philadelphia, 1903), p. 20. Wheeler, the contemporary historian of the company, noted the existence of local branches in many outports but made no mention of Chester. J. Wheeler, *A Treatise of Commerce* (1601), reprinted by *The Facsimile Text Society*, Series 5, 2 (New York, 1931), pp. 19–20.

[2]C. Gross, *op. cit.*, 2, pp. 360–2; B. M. Harl MSS. 2054 fos. 49–50.

[3]Chester R.O. M/L/5/269 1567; B. M. Harl MSS. 2054 f.54, no date, probably belongs to the 1570s.

[4]First manuscript—43 members comprising 16 whose trade is unclear, 17 merchants, 3 drapers, 1 called merchant and draper, 6 others. Second manuscript—53 members comprising 16 whose trade is unclear, 22 merchants, 5 drapers, 2 merchant drapers, 8 others. C. Gross, *op. cit.*, 1, p. 152 suggested that mercers formed a prominent element in the company; this link is not demonstrated by the evidence available.

[5]Wilson I, pp. 1–34 for a discussion of the Chester customs during the period 1301–1558.

[6]*Ibid.*, p. 28.

The assimilation of Chester into the national customs system caused a certain amount of trouble when the city council discovered that the duties Glaseour was demanding were higher than those raised in other ports and higher than those paid previously at Chester. He was demanding duties of 7s. per ton of iron, and 1s. 3d in the pound on all other goods, whereas previously the Chester merchants had paid only 2s. on a ton of iron. The council debated the matter and on 23 April 1560 decided that "Sute for the redres therof should furth with be made to the quenes majestie". William Aldersey and William Jewett were elected to go to London to represent the city and after a wait of 83 days, during which time the matter was considered by the Queen, privy council and other royal officials, they were given a letter to present to Glaseour. This letter told Glaseour that he must bring his duties into line with those demanded in other ports and repay the extra duty he had collected; the duty on iron was to be reduced to 4s a ton and the poundage rate was reduced to a shilling for English and Irish merchants.[1] Henry Hardware, the mayor of Chester, gave this letter to Glaseour on 14 August but, because the order was included in a private letter from the Lord Treasurer, Glaseour said that it did not give him sufficient warrant to discharge the extra duty and declared that until he was given an order signed by the Queen he would continue to tax the merchants at the old rate.[2] Glaseour was true to his word and at the council meeting of 10 January 1561 it was decided that the city should try once again to have this imposition removed. Again William Jewett was elected to go to London in the cause and William Aldersey, mayor of Chester at the time, promised to help as he would be in London on his own business and would not ask for any recompense.[3] On this occasion the efforts of the council were completely successful. An order, signed by the Queen, was sent to the Chester customs officials and stated that the duty on iron was to be reduced to 4s. a ton and the poundage rate for English merchants to a shilling; only alien merchants were to pay the extra poundage.[4]

---

[1]Chester R.O. A/B/1/fos. 95–6.

[2]*Ibid.*, f.96 v.

[3]*Ibid.*, f.98 r and v.

[4]*Ibid.*, fos. 99–101. The costs of William Aldersey and William Jewett during their stay in London for 83 days in 1560 and for a further 42 days in 1561 totalled £40 13s. 8d; these costs included "geiftes and other extra ordinaris" necessary to line the pockets of influential men. This cost was borne by the whole city, assessors being appointed to determine what each citizen should pay. *Ibid.*, fos. 101 v, 103 r & v.

Some years later, in 1573, an attempt was made by the city to reduce further the amount of tonnage and poundage paid at Chester. It was claimed that the payment of these duties had so impoverished the city's merchants that soon there would be hardly anyone left to engage in overseas trade. The council agreed that the mayor, Roger Lea, together with as many councillors and other citizens whom he pleased to name, should travel to London to present this suit at their own costs.[1] This time the city was unsuccessful although later in the year it was still felt that "the same with further travell will be at length obtayned".[2] Such hopes proved desperate for tonnage and poundage continued to be paid in full at Chester throughout Elizabeth's reign. The various attempts to reduce the duties payable at Chester demonstrate the great support which was given, on occasion, to the merchants by the whole city. The influence of the merchants in the council was no doubt largely responsible for these expensive campaigns although it was in the interests of all the citizens to maintain a prosperous merchant community and preserve the importance of the city as a regional market.

During the sixteenth century French wine imported by English merchants bore the heavy duty of 50s. 4d. per tun.[3] This duty was not paid at Chester before 1558[4] and, in the early years of Elizabeth's reign, the Chester merchants resisted attempts to make them pay it; in 1566-7 the Queen was owed nearly £1,100 which represented the unpaid duty on 415 tuns of wine.[5] Unlike the dispute concerning the tonnage and poundage duties, however, little is known about this affair but it must be presumed that the city authorities and the merchants petitioned the Queen and privy council to be freed from this imposition. On 21 May 1567 the Chester merchants were relieved of this payment. This grant stated that the citizens of Chester had, during the previous ten years, lost several notable ships and much merchandise due to both storms and piracy. Because of the inconveniences that would follow if the shipping of the Chester area were to decay too much the merchants of Chester, and others, were excused from paying the arrears of duty they owed the Queen and the Chester merchants were relieved

---

[1]*Ibid.*, f.128.

[2]*Ibid.*, f.132 v.

[3]T. S. Willan, *A Tudor Book of Rates*, pp. xii–xiii. Foreign merchants paid an additional 3s. per tun.

[4]B. M. Harl MSS. 2104 f.312 r & v.

[5]*Ibid.*, 2004 f.730.

of the duty for the rest of her reign.[1] The cost of fighting this cause was borne solely by the merchants; on 6 December 1567 it was estimated that the total cost of the affair amounted to £102 18s. of which about three-quarters had not been paid. This sum was raised by a levy on the 43 members "of the compeny of marchaunt venturers".[2] This levy, of less than £2 per head, was obviously insignificant when compared with the grant which the merchants had received from the Queen. Removal of this duty must have enhanced greatly the profit margin of merchants engaged in the French wine trade and probably contributed materially to the expansion which took place in that trade during the early 1580s once the difficulties of the 1570s had been passed.

II—*Dispute (i)*

The co-operation between the merchants and the city authorities gave way during the late 1570s and 1580s to various disputes which divided the city into two main warring factions. The chief cause of the struggle was the formation of the Spanish Company in 1577 which was joined by some of the Chester merchants who then tried to stop all those who were not members of the company from trading with Spain and Portugal. Those merchants who joined the new company were called the *mere merchants* and their opponents were called the *merchant retailers*.[3] The latter group, comprising the majority of the councillors and all merchants who were not members of the Spanish Company, opposed the mere merchants by using the charters of 1554 and 1559 as their main line of defence. During the 1580s the mere merchants obtained a licence to export calfskins and this also became a matter of conflict between the two groups, intensifying the existing struggle.

The revival of Anglo-Spanish trade by the mid 1570s, after the break in trading relations which followed the seizure of the Genoese bullion at Plymouth and Southampton in 1568, was accompanied by the desire to establish a new trading company to include merchants trading with both Spain and Portugal.[4] Despite some oppo-

---

[1] *Ibid.*, 2004. f 792 v. The original of this grant has not been found; there is no reference to it in the *Calendar of Patent Rolls, Elizabeth I*, IV, 1566–9.

[2] Chester R.O. M/L/5/269.

[3] "Mere merchants" means those who were involved in overseas trade *only* and did not retail. Mere or meare does not refer to the sea as stated by M. J. Groombridge, "Calendar of Chester City Council Minutes 1603–42", *Record Society of Lancashire and Cheshire*, 106 (1956), p. 53.

[4] P.R.O. S.P.D. 12/99/8, 9, November 1574.

sition by a group of London merchants, who objected to the pro-
posed restriction of membership to those who had traded with
Spain and Portugal before 1569, the Spanish Company was
established in 1577 with members from London and some of the
outports including Bristol, Exeter, Southampton and Hull. The
charter laid down that craftsmen or retailers were not to be admitted
to the company and that persons who had traded with Spain and
Portugal during or before 1568 might become members on payment
of a £5 entry fine during the first year, or £10 in subsequent years.[1]

The Chester merchants were allowed by their charters of 1554
and 1559 to trade with both Spain and Portugal but the establishment of the new company made their legal position somewhat
doubtful. Some of the Chester merchants, no doubt partly to try to
clear up any legal difficulties and partly to try to steal a march on
their colleagues, became members of the Spanish Company at an
early date. In August 1578 the president and assistants of the
Spanish Company wrote to several of the Liverpool merchants
saying that they had written to Chester and asked some of the
citizens there to confer with them. This request had been complied
with and the Chester men were said to have had no less care for
Liverpool interests than for their own. The letter also stated that
for the ease and better direction of the Liverpool traders they were
to be joined with Chester as "a member thereof" and were to go to
Chester to confer "with the deputie and assistauntes there".[2] If the
Liverpool merchants refused to co-operate they were to be called to
answer at London.[3] The wording of this letter suggests that the
officers of the Spanish Company had approached some of the
Chester merchants who had willingly joined the Company and then
suggested that the Liverpool merchants should join the Chester
branch. Some time later the mere merchants sent a petition to the
privy council alleging that about two years earlier they, along
with other merchants, had embraced the charter granted to all
those trading with Spain and Portugal.[4]

The Chester merchants wrote to Liverpool in April 1580 to
announce that they had received letters, from the president of the

---

[1]V. M. Shillington and A. B. W. Chapman, *The Commercial Relations of England and
Portugal* (1908), pp. 153-4.

[2]A letter sent from Chester to the Liverpool merchants in 1580 was signed "Your
lovinge frendes Willm Massye, Deputie, Edward Hanmer, Randell Leche,
Thomas Tetlowe, Willm Aldersey, Willm Browne Assistantes." *L.T.B.* II,
pp. 361-2.

[3]*Ibid.*, pp. 360-1.

[4]P.R.O. S.P.D. 15/25/77.

Spanish Company, whereby they were appointed to demand from the Liverpool merchants, who were not members of the Company, such fines as were set down for interlopers in the Spanish and Portuguese trades since January 1578; these fines amounted to twenty five per cent on goods imported from Spain or Portugal. The Liverpool merchants were told to send the money or else appear in person at the court to be held at Chester on 18 April, otherwise it was added "wee muste certifie youre denyall, the which will turne to your further trobles and chardges, for wee have bene alwaies most willinge to have you to conforme yourselves to her Majesties graunte, and joyned yourselves with us at the beginnynge". This letter was carried to Liverpool by "William Helen, the clerke of our societie here in Chester".[1]

The attempt to regulate the trade of Liverpool was not received quietly. Complaint was voiced in Liverpool against "one Wyllyam Massye of Chester, marchaunte, and others his associates there, alleidgine her Majesties graunte of charter incorporatinge theym and others by the tytle of Presidente and felowshippe of marchauntes tradinge Hispanie and Portingale" who were demanding fines from Liverpool merchants and trying to stop their trade with Spain and Portugal. It was agreed by the mayor and council of Liverpool that Robert More should travel to Chester and answer the claims of the Chester merchants and that a petition should be sent to the Queen or privy council.[2] On 2 May 1580 the Chester merchants again wrote to Liverpool. In this letter they referred to the "direction of our president" and said that they had hoped that the Liverpool men either would have gone to Chester or would have sent the money to cover the fines imposed on them. Letters, which had been sent to the Chester branch of the Spanish Company from London, had expressed hopes that the Liverpool interlopers " . . . should eftessoones be curteouslie admonished by us to decist from violatinge her Majesties graunte, and aunswer the penalties thereupon due, otherwise a purservaunte wilbe sent, to your greater chardge". The clerk of the Chester merchants had apparently told his masters that the Liverpool merchants would like "to be a companie" by themselves for Massey and his cosignatories said they would be glad to see this happen and would write letters on behalf of the Liverpool merchants.[3]

---

[1] *L.T.B.* II, pp. 361–2.
[2] *Ibid.*, pp. 358–9.
[3] *Ibid.*, pp. 363–4.

A year later this dispute between the Spanish Company and the Liverpool merchants came to a head. At a Liverpool town council meeting, held on 20 August 1581, it was stated that the attempts against the Liverpool merchants by members of the Company, both of Chester and London, had been revived. Anthony More, John Bryde and Peter Starky had been "taken by pursevaunt, and therupon entred in boundes for theire apparance at Chester, and so to London, to aunswer suche matters as touchinge the premisses shalbe objected against them" and twenty pounds were to be raised in Liverpool to defend this cause.[1] A few weeks later a letter sent from the privy council to the mayor of Chester and to William Massey, William Aldersey and Thomas Tetlow, deputy and assistants of the Spanish Company, ordered that these officials must "forebeare to moleste anie of the citizens or anie of Lirpole until their Lordships have taken other order therin". The mayor was also asked to order the said deputy and assistants, in the name of the privy council, to stop levying impositions and fines on the persons and goods of Liverpool until the further "pleasure and resolucion" of the privy council were known.[2]

But the dispute between Liverpool and the new company was not quite finished. On 18 October 1581 the Liverpool council elected two men who were to travel to London to further the town's cause.[3] The plea made by these representatives to the privy council was successful and on 4 December 1581 Walsingham wrote to the Earl of Derby to inform him of the decision taken in this matter. It was stated that because of the large number of retailers in Liverpool and because there were very few or no mere merchants in that town the president of the Spanish Company had agreed that the retailers should be allowed to continue to trade with foreign parts until there were sufficient merchants to engage solely in foreign trade or until there should be a different order from the privy council. It was added, however, that if Liverpool men, under the cover of this grant, shipped goods for the retailers of Chester they should "ever afterwardes be debarred of the benefite of this tolleracion".[4] The Liverpool merchants and retailers had managed finally to overthrow the control of the Spanish Company. It is interesting to note that this settlement of the Liverpool problem was

---

[1] *Ibid.*, pp. 385–6.
[2] Morris, pp. 464–5; *A.P.C.* XIII, pp. 206–8.
[3] *L.T.B.* II, pp. 390–1.
[4] *Ibid.*, pp. 404–5.

very similar to the solution laid down for Chester some years later.[1]

It was not only at Liverpool, however, that the establishment of the Spanish Company was used as a lever in an attempt to exclude retailers from overseas trade. As early as 1577 a letter was despatched to Bristol from the privy council ordering retailers to stop trading with Spain.[2] One of the Bristol merchants who refused to comply was ordered, in December 1578, to appear before the privy council if he still proved to be obstinate. This was not so much an attempt to exclude the Bristolian from trading with Spain and Portugal as an attempt to make him give up his retailing business; other merchants, who presumably had been combining retailing with overseas trade before 1577, were to be allowed to trade if they gave up retailing.[3]

At Chester it was this same problem which caused the trouble. The Chester merchants who attempted to oust retailers and non-members of the company in Liverpool from the trade with Spain and Portugal naturally pursued the same policy in their own port. In an undated petition to the privy council the mere merchants stated that "about two yeres past or more they duetifullie ymbraced hir majesties gracious Chartre granted generallie to all merchantes tradinge Spaine and Portingale" and added that this had led to controversy in the city. They alleged that certain retailers and artificers were not content to live by their trades but had procured the aid of the city authorities and, using the charter of 1554 to defend their actions, had taken liberty to do as they pleased to the detriment of the mere merchants. The privy council was asked to stop the retailers and artificers from trading or, alternatively, if they were to be allowed to trade then the merchants wished to be allowed to retail.[4] A counter petition was sent to the privy council at about the same time by the merchant retailers. They said that the mere merchants had always been retailers, as well as wholesalers, and that this had never been denied to them. The petitioners therefore begged that they should be troubled no more over this matter but be allowed to retail and to trade overseas.[5] At this early stage in the dispute the two sides appear to have been drawing towards an

---

[1]See below pp. 101-2.

[2]*A.P.C.* X, p. 16.

[3]*Ibid.*, pp. 408-9.

[4]P.R.O. S.P.D. 15/25/77. Probably 1579 or 1580.

[5]*Ibid.*, 15/26/6.

agreement but, because both sides distrusted each other and continually hoped to gain the upper hand, the final settlement was postponed for some ten years.

The dispute between the city authorities and the mere merchants was not fought on purely economic grounds. In March 1581, when the council decided to make the dispute with the Spanish Company a "cities cause" and sent a petition to the privy council, reference was made to "William Massie, Thomas Tetlowe, and others of this citie beinge against the chartres of this citie".[1] The council felt that the prerogative of the city was involved and was opposed to an outside merchant body having a branch at Chester to regulate the trade of the port in much the same way that it had opposed the establishment of the original company in 1554. The fear of the damage that might be done to the city's authority and the fact that the retailers and craftsmen outnumbered the mere merchants in the council will explain why the mayor and council joined the retailers in opposition to the mere merchants.

Both factions in the dispute became very active during the mayoralty of Richard Bavand in 1581–2 and the timing of this increase in activity was no mere coincidence. In an undated petition to Walsingham the mere merchants called their mayor "a man notorious in many professions"[2] and some years later a Mr. Bavand was referred to as an ironmonger, vintner, mercer and retailer of many commodities.[3] Richard Bavand traded with Spain during the 1560s and 1570s but in the early 1580s he participated only in the Irish and coasting trades. It may be that Bavand, who was a member of the original merchant company of Chester,[4] was kept out of the Spanish trade by members of the Chester branch of the Spanish Company. He would thus be as keen as anyone to remove the restrictions imposed by that body.

The privy council sent a letter to Chester in September 1581 ordering the city council to send two representatives to London along with the merchants' charter of 1554, the city charter and any other evidence which supported their claims against the mere merchants and Spanish Company. Representatives of the mere merchants were also summoned to London and the whole affair

---

[1] Morris, p. 464.

[2] P.R.O. S.P.D. 12/129/53 No date, but almost certainly 1582 ante 6 July.

[3] *Ibid.*, 15/31/28. No date, probably 1589. Mr. Bavand was called the father-in-law of David Lloyd. See the copy of Lloyd's will which refers to Richard Bavand his father-in-law. B. M. Harl. MSS. 1991 fos. 176–9.

[4] Chester R.O. M/L/5/269; B. M. Harl. MSS. 2054 f.54.

was to be submitted to legal experts. In the meantime, however, before a final decision could be made, the trade with Spain and Portugal was to be thrown open.[1] A month later the mayor wrote to the Earl of Leicester, who was the chamberlain of Chester, to try to get his support in the dispute. He told Leicester that the council had agreed to appoint Robert Dodd, his nominee, as the city's swordbearer and added that Dodd had been made a freeman of Chester. In return the mayor solicited Leicester's help in the battle against the "Compeny of merchantes tradinge Spayne and Portingall".[2]

As promised, the privy council referred the dispute to its legal advisors[3]—the Attorney General, the Lord Chief Justice and the Master of the Rolls—who reported back on 1 December 1581. After interviewing all the parties concerned they concluded that the Spanish Company by making orders to bind the Chester merchant company of 1554 and attempting to "putte all that use retaylinge of wares in Chester and other places from their trafique as merchauntes venterers" was doing "more then theye maye doe by vertue of theire said charter". They felt that "if retailers of suche poore cities and townes, where smale trade of merchaundizes is used, shoulde be putt from theire trade of shipping, it woulde be a greate decaye to the same poore cities and townes".[4] As was mentioned earlier this advice was taken in relation to the dispute at Liverpool but the Spanish Company was more firmly entrenched at Chester where, despite this ruling, the dispute dragged on.

Early in April 1582 the city council decided to try to break the deadlock by obtaining a new charter for the merchant company which would be for the benefit of the whole city and replace the charter of 1554 which was felt to be imperfect. At the same meeting it was disclosed that the mere merchants had voiced their complaints before certain commissioners appointed by the privy council. The merchants had asked for three concessions; that they should be allowed to retail if the retailers were allowed to trade overseas, that the whole city should bear the costs of the mere merchants as well as those of the retailers, and that if their costs were not paid they should not be asked to contribute towards the costs of the retailers.

---

[1]Morris, pp. 464–5; *A.P.C.* XIII, pp. 206–8. On 26 October 1581 the council elected John Hanky, an alderman and member of the 1554 company, and Robert Brocke, gentleman, to go to London. Morris, p. 466; Chester R.O. A/B/1/f.183.

[2]Chester R.O. M/L/5/32.

[3]*A.P.C.* XIII, p. 255.

[4]*L.T.B.* II, pp. 403–4; P.R.O. S.P.D. 12/150/79.

The city council said that it agreed to the first two requests and referred the third to the mayor's consideration.[1]

The commissioners to whom the mere merchants had voiced their grievances were Christopher Goodman, John Reynolds and Henry Hardware who reported to Walsingham on 2 May.[2] The retailers had told the commissioners that they were satisfied with the resolutions set down by the privy council's legal advisors and were willing to allow the mere merchants to retail. The mere merchants, on the other hand, were not so satisfied with the opinions expressed against the Spanish Company and refused to yield until directly ordered to do so by the privy council. This refusal to give ground was probably due in part to the refusal of the city council to bear the costs of the merchants or make any repayment of the sums levied on them towards the costs of the retailers; despite the decision taken by the council on 6 April Richard Bavand had informed the commissioners that the council would not agree to these points. The commissioners ended, sadly, by stating that they could not find a way to resolve the controversy but added that if a speedy remedy could be set down by the privy council it would be to the general good of the whole city.[3]

After the commissioners had made their report the mere merchants sent a petition to Walsingham. Reminding him that they had told him at the end of the previous Michaelmas Term of their "greivous estate" they alleged that they were content to follow their trade of merchandise only and that the mayor had set men, of any occupation, at liberty to trade and adventure overseas. They said that

> "their sute was then repugned against by the saide nowe Maior and serten other Retaylors & handycraftesmen who (not respectinge a comon wealth but their owne private comoditie) toke holde (Usurpinglie) of a chartre graunted frome queene Mary, not to theym but to the Merchauntes which hath not of longe

---

[1]Chester R.O. A/B/1/fos. 184v–185; Morris, p. 466.

[2]Henry Hardware was a draper who became a freeman of Chester in 1546 and was mayor of the city in 1559–60 and 1575–6. The Henry Hardware who was mayor in 1599–1600 was probably his son who became a freeman of the city in 1583. *F.R.*, pp. 25, 57; Morris, p. 583. Christopher Goodman, who was a personal friend of John Knox and one of the authors of the Genevan Bible, had made his peace with the Elizabethan church and at the time of this commission was Dean of Chester. He was born in about 1519, died in 1603 and was probably the nephew of Adam Goodman and cousin of William Goodman, both of whom traded with the continent in Elizabeth's reign.

J. E. Bailey, "Christopher Goodman, a native of Chester", *Journal of the Chester Archaeological and Historic Society*, N.S. I (1887) pp. 138–9 151.

[3]P.R.O. S.P.D. 12/153/33.

tyme byn put in execution for the ymperfection thereof. And so resistinge hir majestes generall Chartre latelie graunted to all subiectes tradinge Spaine and Portingale . . . certen Retailors and handycraftesmen . . . have and do assemble theymselves togither, as it were into a fellowshipp, and have and do admitt men not of merchauntes professions"

which was a great hindrance to the petitioners and had led to the overthrow of the navy at Chester. The mere merchants said that they themselves were content "to live symplie in the compas of their owne professions" and asked Walsingham to help them so that the privy council would forbid retailers to be merchants unless they stopped retailing. The old plea, that the mere merchants should be allowed to retail if it were decided that the retailers and handi-craftsmen could be merchants, was repeated.[1]

At the Chester council meeting of the 6 July 1582 a copy of this so-called "sclanderous bill . . . exhibited to sir Frauncis Walsing-ham" was read out. The council ordered that the mere merchants should have a week to consider how far their actions were contrary to their oaths taken in the city and to decide whether or not they would submit themselves and become good citizens or else be "warned to be disfranchised and then to be fyned".[2] When the council met a week later it was decided that the punishment of William Massey, Thomas Tetlow, William Aldersey, William Browne and Peter Mainwaring should be postponed because the whole matter was being considered by the privy council.[3]

The privy council once again delegated its authority to commis-sioners and at the Chester council meeting of 15 August 1582 it was decided that the merchant retailers should be represented by ten citizens including "Mr. Rich. Birkened recorder, Mr. Randull Hurleston, Mr. John Reignoldes esquires lerned in the lawes".[4] Again no workable solution was reached for at the council meeting of 25 March 1583 it was decided once more who should appear before the commissioners. For the retailers, the recorder, Richard Bavand, Robert Brocke and Mr. Mountford were appointed while William Massey, Thomas Tetlow, William Browne and William

---

[1]*Ibid.* 12/129/53. Undated but ante 6 July 1582 because a copy of this petition was shown to the Chester council on that day. Morris p. 466.

[2]Chester R.O. A/B/1/f. 185 r & v. Morris p. 466.

[3]Chester R.O. A/B/1/f.186.

[4]*Ibid.* f. 186 v. It will be noticed that "John Reignoldes" was one of the commis-sioners to whom the dispute was referred earlier in the year.

Aldersey, who volunteered to appear for themselves and for the rest of the mere merchants were likewise accepted.[1]

III—*The struggle for recompense*

At this point it is necessary to break away from the dispute over the machinations of the Spanish Company and its Chester members to examine the different ways in which the Chester merchants sought to recoup the heavy losses they sustained during the 1570s. At first the merchants attempted to obtain restitution from the pirates who had plundered their ships and from merchants of the towns to which the pirates were believed to belong. Thus in 1575 complaints from the citizens of Chester and Bristol about acts of piracy committed by some men of St. Malo were referred, by the privy council, to the Judge of the Admiralty Court. These alleged acts of piracy were to be investigated and, if they were found to be true, the French ambassador was to be informed.[2] Some months later a "letter of assistaunce of processe of thadmiraltie" was given to Foulk Aldersey for the piracy committed on the *Bear Warwick* by the pirates of St. Malo.[3] These efforts were successful initially for at about this time William Michelot, a merchant of St. Malo, was arrested by some unnamed Chester citizens in an action for £400 because of an alleged incident involving some pirates of St. Malo. Michelot pleaded innocence claiming that he was in England at the time when these piracies were committed.[4] He also seems to have been held responsible for the capture of the *Bear Warwick;* by 20 May 1579 Michelot had been condemned in the High Court of Admiralty, at the suit of Foulk Aldersey and Peter Newall, for a sum of £3,000 to be paid to them in recompense for the £5,000 worth of damage done by pirates of St. Malo. But the "law's delay" took its toll; Michelot appealed against the sentence and the Chester merchants were said to be almost ruined.[5] By appealing to the

---

[1] *Ibid.* f.190. It is interesting to note that Bavand and Mountford often traded in partnership during the 1570's and early 1580's, especially in the French wine trade. It will be remembered that Mountford was harsh in his criticism of his fellow merchants during the investigation into smuggling offences at Chester. See above p. 62.

[2] *A.P.C.* IX pp. 5–6.

[3] *Ibid.*, p. 62.

[4] P.R.O. S.P.D. 12/106/10.

[5] *A.P.C.* XI p. 131. A merchant's factor, Bernard Jourdain of St. Malo, was arrested at the suit of the Chester merchants in 1577. Jourdain was given some help by Michelot but whether or not the Chester merchants received any satisfaction from this arrest does not emerge. C. E. Hughes, "Wales and Piracy", *op. cit.*, pp. 162–4.

Court of Chancery Michelot escaped from the fine of £400;[1] whether
or not he escaped payment of the larger sum does not appear, but
it seems likely that he did.

The losses claimed by the Chester merchants, due to piracy and
shipwreck, amounted to more than £20,000 by 1580 and at about
that time the merchants and citizens sent a petition to the privy
council asking that body to persuade the Queen to relieve their
decayed state. Seven specific privileges were asked for in this petition.
First it was asked that the ambassador should approach the French
king and try to obtain restitution for the piracies committed by his
subjects. It was asked also that citizens of Chester should be relieved
from all customs and that foreigners should pay their customs to the
use of the city, or else that Cestrians should be discharged until
their fortunes were restored. A licence to export calfskins was sought
and also a licence to transport 200 packs of yarn a year from Ireland.
The petitioners wanted Chester to be made the staple for Manchester cottons and a request was made that the transportation of
copper mined by the Mines Royal Company should be conducted
only by Chester merchants and in Chester ships. Lastly it was
hoped that the Queen would build a haven at Chester at her own
cost.[2] Many of the points asked for in the above petition were laid
down again in another undated manuscript. In addition, however,
it was suggested that the Chester causeway should be destroyed so
that the river could have its "ffrye course with great lande waters
violently to scoure the haven"; windmills, it was suggested, could
provide the necessary power for grinding corn. Again a licence to
import linen yarn was asked for and it was hoped that they could
"begin a trade of endraperye of linen, to the avoiding of dire
purchasing of foreign labour", at Chester. The pleas concerning
the restoration of the haven, Manchester cottons, copper and the
securing of restitution from the French were repeated.[3]

At about the same time Peter Newall, Foulk and William
Aldersey, Robert Dryhurst, Thomas Tetlow and John Fletcher, who
had all lost heavily when the *Bear Warwick* was captured,[4] became
suitors to the privy council. These merchants mentioned the
petition that they had sent to the Queen the previous August, in
which they had asked for recompense for their losses, when they had

---

[1] P.R.O. S.P.D. 12/229/55.

[2] *Ibid.*, 15/27/35. No date probably 1579–80.

[3] *Ibid.*, 12/158/3. No date, but before 8 October 1581 for it deals with matters then
dealt with by the privy council.

[4] Morris, p. 472.

been asked to wait until the Queen heard what recompense was to be given to the merchants from France. In this new petition these Chester merchants asked either for letters of marque to recompense themselves from the French or to be allowed to take a ship belonging to St. Malo or Brittany found in one of the Queen's ports. If these schemes were not approved by the privy council then the merchants asked for whatever satisfaction should be thought meet.[1]

Another two, very similar, undated petitions were sent to the privy council from Chester. In neither of the petitions was any particular privilege asked for; both merely pointed out that Chester was in great difficulties because of piracy, shipwreck and the decay of the haven. It was stated that where there had once been "10 or 12 sealles of shippes and tow hundrethe mariners" there was not one ship left and not above four able mariners,[2] and that therefore the coast around Chester had become defenceless. It was felt that the government could not allow this decay to continue because Chester was the main port for the embarkation of troops going to Ireland and a bulwark against Wales for, it was added, "since suche tymes as have bene may be agayne . . . walles maye rebell". The important trade which Chester merchants had previously conducted with France, Spain, Portugal and Ireland was said to be decayed and some merchants were said to "kepe (to) theire owne housses ffor ffyre of the . . . extremities of theire Creditours". Some of the citizens were said to avoid becoming city officials because of the expense and general opinion in the city considered that "yt ys tyme to Complayne, and to shewe oure nakednes, with our woundes blydinge, washinge them with the tyrres of misery, untyll the surgione have geven us Commfforte of relyffe".[3]

There is no doubt that these two petitions paint a rather too gloomy picture of Chester's fortunes in the early 1580s, but there is also little doubt that the Chester merchants and citizens had suffered quite heavy financial losses. The loss of ships and commodities worth more than £20,000 must have been a harsh blow to many of the Chester merchants; but Elizabethan trade was often a hazardous affair as the Hull merchants, who lost goods worth £23,000 in a shorter period than the Chester merchants had suffered their

---

[1] P.R.O. S.P.D. 15/27/89. Probably 1580.

[2] They probably meant the larger ships capable of regular voyages to France and Spain.

[3] P.R.O. S.P.D. 12/110/46, 158/4. No dates but they clearly date from the early 1580s.

losses, discovered.[1] Also the silting of the Dee was a constant inconvenience to the citizens and merchants of Chester and the haven, a source of trouble for so many years, was a continual drain on the resources of the city and ultimately proved a complete failure. It is clear, however, that the privy council thought that the fortunes of Chester were in decline. In a letter to the mayor of Chester, dated 26 February 1581, it was stated that "diverse of the cittie of Chester are within theise fewe yeares paste fallen into povertie" and it was decided that, as the Queen intended to relieve the Cestrians, "the rigor of their creditours, their executours and atturnies attempting the extremitie of the lawe againste them" should be stayed. Any creditors who refused to wait for their money were to be brought to the notice of the privy council who would deal with them.[2]

On 8 October 1581 the privy council set down its opinion concerning the seven concessions that had been asked for earlier by the merchants and citizens of Chester. To the first request the privy council said that the Cestrians should prove the spoils done by the French in the Court of Admiralty and then the proofs would be sent to the Queen's ambassador in France who would deal with the French king for restitution. The privy council was favourable to three demands of the Chester merchants and citizens. It was thought good that Chester should be the staple for Manchester cottons for seven years, and a note was made beside the petition to export calfskins to the effect that permission should be granted to export 500 dickers of calfskins, paying a duty of 1s 8d. a dicker, for an unspecified number of years. Only the mere merchants, however, were to be allowed to export calfskins. The privy council also thought that the Queen should give some assistance towards building the haven. On the other hand it was thought inexpedient that the Cestrians should be granted any relief from customs, and it was decided that further advice should be sought from the Lord Deputy of Ireland and the Mines Royal Company before a decision was made about the transportation of linen yarn and copper respectively.[3]

---

[1]M. Oppenheim, *A History of the Administration of the Royal Navy and of Merchant Shipping in Relation to the Navy* (1896), I, p. 173. The Southampton merchants lost £12,000 through shipwreck and piracy during the four years before 1582. Wiggs, *op. cit.*, p. 54.

[2]*A.P.C.* XII , pp. 342–3.

[3]P.R.O. S.P.D. 12/150/38. This manuscript mentions 300 packs of linen yarn rather than 200 packs mentioned in S.P.D. 15/27/35.

Some time later another petition was sent to the privy council from Chester. Some of the Chester citizens had travelled to discover the opinions of the Lord Deputy of Ireland and the Mines Royal Company and had been told that it was not convenient that they should be granted the concessions concerning linen yarn and copper. Other concessions were therefore asked for in this new petition. The ruinous state of the haven, which was said to have cost £3,000 to that date, was stressed and, to help towards the cost of finishing it, a licence to export 500 tuns of beer a year or a certain quantity of grain, duty free, was requested. It was also hoped that the statute of sewers would be put into operation to pull up fishyards and other impediments in the river that destroyed young fishes and wrecked many boats and lighters. A licence was sought to export 600 dickers of calfskins a year which were to be provided within fifty miles of Chester. Again letters of marque, or else permission to confiscate goods belonging to Brittany merchants, were asked for because the Chester merchants had heard that the French king was not willing to help them to obtain satisfaction for the losses thay had suffered.[1] Another very similar petition was sent to the privy council, the main difference from the above petition being that the request to export calfskins was more ambitious in that it was hoped that the Cestrians would be allowed to transport yearly for twelve years 1,000 dickers of calfskins paying 1s. a dicker to the Queen.[2]

Meanwhile, the Chester merchants had continued in their efforts to obtain restitution from the French. In April 1582 Walsingham received two letters on this subject from Paris.[3] The first of these informed him that the suit of the Chester merchants had been recommended to the English ambassador, Sir Henry Cobham,[4] who agreed to help although he seemed to have little hope of success. The second letter was from Cobham himself who said that he had seen a certain M. Pinard, a Frenchman, and had recommended to him the causes of the Chester merchants. Pinard had promised to do what he could and apparently intended to place the matter before the king. Cobham wrote to Walsingham again on 14 May to say that the French king had written to the governors of the three towns to which the pirates belonged to see that restitution was made to the Chester merchants.[5] This letter ended with

[1] *Ibid.*, 12/150/36.

[2] *Ibid.*, 12/150/37.

[3] *Ibid.*, 15/27A/70. *Cal. S.P. Foreign*, 1581–2, p. 640.
[4] Cobham was English ambassador resident at Paris during 1579–83. *D.N.B.*
[5] *Cal. S.P. Foreign*, *1582, p.* 31.

a promise that Cobham would further this suit by all the means he could devise. Walsingham replied on 7 June 1582 and told Cobham that he had seen the Chester merchants and had told them of Cobham's efforts on their behalf. He had advised the Chester merchants to send some direction to a certain Marbury for following up their suit and also to send some reasonable allowance for his "travell" therein. The Chester merchants were said to be discouraged because they had had little return so far for the money they had expended, but Walsingham meant to see whether he could persuade them differently.[1] Charles Marbury, an Englishman who had also suffered at the hands of French pirates, was in Paris at that time attempting to gain some recompense for his losses,[2] but he did not act as agent for the Chester merchants for very long. He soon resigned this charge, on Cobham's advice, to a Frenchman who was a friend of the latter and seemed more fit to further the cause of the Chester merchants.[3]

The discouraged attitude of the Chester merchants seems to have been justified for there is no evidence that they gained any recompense from the French. Similarly, it seems likely that William Ratcliffe failed to obtain satisfaction from the Spanish. He sent a petition to the privy council whereby he hoped to gain some relief for the double piracy committed on his ship, the *Sunday* of Chester, in 1579. Ratcliffe asked for letters of marque against the inhabitants of Corunna and neighbouring towns or else a grant of such pirates' goods brought to England that he could discover to the value of his losses.[4] There is in fact no evidence that the merchants received any direct recompense for their losses.

Another way that the Cestrians thought they might be able to relieve their fortunes was by making Chester the staple for Welsh cottons. In the sixteenth century Welsh cloth was taken first to Oswestry and then to Shrewsbury where much of it was finished. From there most of the cloth was sent overland to London and marketed at Blackwell Hall before being sent to the continent or distributed for consumption at home. The bulk of the Welsh cloth sent to London was exported to France, and particularly to Rouen.[5]

[1] *Ibid.*, pp. 71–2.
[2] *Ibid.*, p. 31. He was author of one of the letters sent to Walsingham in April. P.R.O. S.P.D. 15/27A/70.
[3] *Ibid.*, 15/27A/109.
[4] *Ibid.*, 12/157 /50.
[5] T. C. Mendenhall, *The Shrewsbury Drapers and the Welsh Wool Trade in the Sixteenth and Seventeenth Centuries* (Oxford, 1953), chapters 2 & 3.

In the early 1580s a petition was sent to the privy council from Chester to ask that a staple for Welsh cottons should be established in that city. Arguments, rehearsed in earlier petitions, about the need to maintain Chester were again repeated and it was also argued that because of other resources, due to its border location, Shrewsbury did not really need the trade. The most interesting feature of this petition is the dislike, manifested by the Cestrians, of the great concentration of trade through London. It was stated that "To bring all trades, all shippinge, and all gaynes to Londone ys not the best course. And in respecte of the state, yt ys like As yf all the Ordenance and men in A sorte were brought to one bulwarke, While all other partes remayne weike and unmaned".[1] It has been suggested that this petition had nothing but Chester's plight to recommend it,[2] and indeed this seems to have been the case for Chester was certainly badly placed for trade with Rouen.

This attempt to make Chester the staple for Welsh cottons provoked a counter petition from Shrewsbury, "the self-appointed and acknowledged champion of the existing order".[3] The citizens of Shrewsbury had no objection to the exportation of Welsh cloth through Chester; their objection was against Chester being made the sole port through which this trade could be conducted. It was argued that the journey from Shrewsbury to Rouen via Chester would be more expensive and more dangerous than the established route. The poverty of the trade, it was alleged, demanded a quick return which Chester was not equipped to give, and it was added that "the povertie of Wales cannot tarie for the enriching of Chester".[4] The sum of the objections lodged by Shrewsbury was that Chester "lacked the location, the merchants, the resources to act as the intermediary between Welsh cloth manufacture and its ultimate market abroad".[5]

On 6 January 1583 the privy council again considered the privileges asked for by the inhabitants of Chester, and once again the council could see no reason why Chester should not be established as the staple for Manchester cottons. There is no evidence, however, to suggest that Chester ever received such a licence; indeed the export of Manchester cottons to the continent was almost non-

[1] *Tudor Economic Documents, op. cit.*, 1, pp. 199–203. Mendenhall, *op. cit.*, pp. 133–4.
[2] *Ibid.*, p. 135.
[3] *Ibid.*, p. 134.
[4] *Tudor Economic Documents, op. cit.*, pp. 203–12.
[5] Mendenhall, *op. cit.*, p. 134.

existent after the mid 1580s. The privy council also thought it convenient that the "myre merchauntes of Chester, incorporate to the merchauntes of lonndon tradinge spaygne and portingale" should be granted a licence to export calfskins. This licence was to allow the merchants to export 12,000 dickers of calfskins paying duty of 1*s.* per dicker. It will be seen later that this was the final form of the licence granted to the Chester merchants twenty-one months later. The privy council also considered the plea to make Chester the staple for Welsh cloth. The council must have decided at an earlier meeting to allow Chester to become the staple for at least a part the Welsh cloth trade; the LordChancellor alleged that Shrewsbury had not presented a sufficiently good argument to persuade the council to revoke its first decree for stapling the North Welsh friezes at Chester. Even so, Burghley ordered that some citizens of Shrewsbury should be sent for so that the council could hear what further arguments they could put forward.[1] In the end, however, the whole dispute was won by the citizens of Shrewsbury and Chester did not become the staple for any part of the Welsh cloth trade.[2] Finally, at this meeting of 6 January, it was decided by the privy council that a commission of sewers should be set up, but as Burghley was taking the names of the commissioners the whole council was called before the Queen and this matter was not concluded.[3]

The licence to export calfskins was granted to the Chester merchants on 7 September 1584. It was stated that the Chester merchants had in the past maintained good ships whereby the Queen's affairs in Ireland had been aided and that they had suffered great losses by piracy and shipwreck and therefore would be able to maintain themselves only with the Queen's help. The licence was to allow "the meere marchantes . . . using onelye the feates of marchandyzes by venturing by sea and sale in grosse and not by retayling and nowe being members of the bodye corporate of the Presydent assistantes and fellowshyppe of marchauntes of Spayne and Portingale" to carry out of Chester, or her members, 10,000 dickers of calfskins within 12 years. A duty of 1*s.* per dicker was to be levied and the number of calfskins shipped from Chester was to be entered in the port books and also on the back of the licence. The mere merchants were authorised to search any ship in the port of Chester, or her members, and confiscate any leather or calfskins

---

[1]P.R.O. S.P.D. 12/158/2.

[2]*A.P.C.*, 1613–14, pp. 34–40. Mendenhall, *op. cit.*, p. 135.

[3]P.R.O. S.P.D. 12/158/2.

waiting to be unlawfully exported. Such confiscated wares were to be divided into three parts; one part was to be given to the Queen, one part to the mere merchants and the third part to the mayor of Chester for the repair of the decayed haven. Only the mere merchants were to have the benefit of this licence which was to be kept in a chest with two locks; the key of one of these locks was to be kept by the deputy of the merchant company and the other was to be kept by another member of the company who was to be elected, from time to time, by the mere merchants. It was also laid down that any mere merchant who did not obey an order laid down by the company, or by the majority of the mere merchants in assembly, was to be excluded from the benefit of the licence until he should submit himself to orders laid down by his fellow merchants. The offending merchant was also to be fined and committed to the city prison until the fine was fully paid.[1]

A similar licence to export calfskins was also granted to Peter Newall, one of the Chester merchants, on the same day. He was granted the privilege of exporting 2,000 dickers of calfskins, over a period of 12 years, from the ports of Chester, Bristol, Bridgwater, Barnstaple and their members. He also was to pay a duty of 1s. per dicker on the skins he exported. Newall was to be allowed to search ships in any of these ports and confiscate calfskins waiting to be unlawfully exported; half the proceeds of such discoveries were to go to the Queen and half to Newall.[2]

IV—*Dispute (ii)*

The licence to export calfskins which was granted to the mere merchants not only gave them a good opportunity to recoup their losses but also provided a strong buttress to their power in their struggle with the merchant retailers of the city. They were not, however, allowed to enjoy this new privilege quietly. The mayor, council and merchant retailers manifested an instant dislike for the monopoly which the mere merchants were to exercise over the licence and joined this new grievance to the old grievances they had cultivated over the previous seven years.

Needless to say, the city authorities and merchant retailers were extremely dissatisfied with the licence which had been granted to Peter Newall. It is clear from an entry in the Assembly Book, for

---

[1] P.R.O. Patent Rolls, 26 Elizabeth, part 7, mem. 1–3.

[2] *Ibid.*, mem. 3–4. Newall later sold his licence to some Bristol merchants so that he could pay his debts. P.R.O. S.P.D. 12/185/71.

20 March 1581, that Peter Newall was not regarded merely as an agent for the mere merchants. Newall was alleged to have made many petitions, before that date, to obtain some authority from the council in suing for some licence before the privy council for the relief of the "poore decayed estate of this Citie". He had also asked for some money to help to pay for the journey he was about to make to London in this matter. The council agreed that Newall should have the city's authority in the prosecution of this suit and ordered him to report, from time to time, and inform the recorder of Chester of his proceedings. To defray his charges the assembly granted £40 which was to be levied on the whole city.[1] It was with some justification, therefore, that the mayor protested when Newall obtained the calfskin licence solely for the benefit of the mere merchants and himself. At a council meeting held in the early part of 1585 the mayor ordered Peter Newall to show the licence, which he alleged had been obtained, for exporting calfskins. Newall, probably realising the commotion that would ensue if the licence were read before the whole council, said he would show the licence to the customs officers, as was required, and also agreed to show it to the mayor and recorder. He refused, however, to show it to the rest of the council.[2]

For some reason both the licence given to the mere merchants and the licence given to Peter Newall were renewed in 1586.[3] These new licences were almost identical to the licences granted eighteen months earlier, the only difference being in Peter Newall's grant. In the second licence he was authorised to export calfskins from Bristol, Bridgwater, Barnstaple and Chepstow, whereas in the earlier licence he had been authorised to ship calfskins from Bristol, Bridgwater, Barnstaple and Chester.[4] The original licences were crossed out and on the back of the licence to the mere merchants there is an interesting statement; William Massey, William Aldersey, Foulk Aldersey, Thomas Tetlow, Richard Knee and the two Richard Rathbones, acting for themselves and other mere merchants, appointed Peter Newall their "true and leafull attornie to yeld surrender and deliver upp to her majesties use the sayd lettres patentes". This statement was sealed and delivered on 26 July 1586 in the presence of Solomon Smith, Richard Weaver, John Wright

---

[1]Chester R.O.A/B/1/f180.

[2]*Ibid.*, f. 197v.

[3]P.R.O. Patent Rolls, 28 Elizabeth, part 1, mem. 5—11. 4 March 1586.

[4]*Ibid.*, 26 Elizabeth, part 7, mem. 3–4.

and William Helen, all of whom were obviously members of the mere merchants' party.[1]

Unfortunately no more information is available about the course of the dispute between the two main factions at Chester during the two years following the renewal of these licences. It is obvious, however, that this dispute did not lie dormant for on 14 December 1588 Walsingham wrote to the mayor of Chester and ordered that Peter Newall and David Lloyd on the one side and representatives of the mere merchants on the other side should appear before the privy council.[2] Walsingham seems to have been misinformed about the allegiances of various Chester citizens for Newall was a mere merchant whereas David Lloyd supported the retailers and city authorities. At a council meeting held on 25 February 1589 Walsingham's letter was discussed and the complaints of the city were debated. The council condemned the actions of Peter Newall who, they said, had agreed to present to the privy council the suit for a licence to export calfskins which was to be for the benefit of the whole city and had received money from the city towards his costs. But, as we have seen, the licence had been procured solely for the benefit of the mere merchants. The council decided to send a petition to the privy council to try either to transfer the benefit of the licence to all the free citizens of Chester, or else to obtain a new licence of which all could partake. It was also agreed that letters should be written to individual members of the privy council, and especially to the Earl of Derby, to canvass support for this suit. Finally it was arranged that Peter Newall and William Aldersey for the mere merchants and David Lloyd and Richard Bavand for the other side should go to London and be available for consultation from 5 March 1589.[3] A letter was written to Walsingham to inform him of the decisions taken by the council that day.[4]

A few weeks later the mayor and some of his brethren wrote again to Walsingham. The four Chester representatives had gone up to London as agreed and Lloyd and Bavand had become suitors to Walsingham in an attempt to reform the calfskin licence. But apparently Peter Newall denied that Bavand had been sent by the council for that purpose. The mayor wished Walsingham to know that Bavand had been appointed by the whole council to represent

---

[1] *Ibid.*, mem. 1.
[2] Chester R.O. M/L/5/81.
[3] *Ibid.*, A/B/1/f.219v.
[4] *Ibid.*, M/L/5/251.

the citizens of Chester and hoped that Walsingham would be favourable to the city and further the suit presented by Lloyd and Bavand.[1]

The privy council appointed a committee of four London merchants to inquire into the dispute. The members of this committee, Hugh Offley and Richard Saltonstall, both aldermen and sheriffs of London, Thomas Aldersey and Thomas Bromley, reported back to the privy council on 18 April 1589.[2] Two of these merchants, Hugh Offley and Thomas Aldersey, had close connections with the city and county of Chester and it was probably for this reason that they were chosen to sit on the committee.[3] It was the opinion of these London merchants that because those called mere merchants "are so fewe as they can not mayntaine soche beneficyall trad as were mete" they should be allowed to retail. They also thought that those retailers who were known to have used the "trayd of merchandize heretofore" should be allowed to be both retailers and merchants. Further, their opinion was that "where there are now two sortes of marchantes holdinge by severall grantes, yt were very fytt they shoulde be unityd into one company and to be ruled by one ordar and governement" and that they should all enjoy the licence to export calfskins. Finally, they thought that if an order were laid down in this matter by the privy council it would be obeyed by both parties.

The mere merchants studied the proposals made by the four London merchants and informed the mayor of their opinions on 30 April 1589. The suggestion that they should be allowed to retail was welcomed and it was agreed that those retailers who had been merchants before should be allowed to act as both merchants and retailers. It is obvious that the mere merchants hoped to restrict the number of retailers who were to be allowed to trade for they wanted the names of those retailers who had acted as merchants previously to be written down, presumably to facilitate the exclusion of others. The mere merchants were also in favour of a merger

---

[1] P.R.O. S.P.D. 12/223/82.

[2] *Ibid.*, 12/223/93. See Chester R.O. M/L/5/252 for a copy of this report.

[3] Hugh Offley, one of the sons of William Offley who migrated to Chester from Stafford, followed some of his brothers to London where he became a member of the Merchant Adventurers' Company. Thomas Aldersey, who was a native of Bunbury in Cheshire and related to the Chester Alderseys, was Member of Parliament for London in 1572 and 1581 and served as an alderman of London from 1581 to 1588. T. S. Willan, *The Muscovy Merchants of 1555* (Manchester, 1953), p. 14; G. C. Bower, "A Manuscript Relating to the Family of Offley", *The Genealogist*, 19 (1903), pp. 83, 87–8; W. K. Jordan, *The Charities of London 1480–1660* (1960), pp. 103–4, 169.

of the two merchant companies but took this to mean that those retailers who were to be allowed to trade should join the Spanish Company. If the merger failed to take this form the mere merchants thought that a new company would have to be formed and a new licence to export calfskins obtained which, they thought, could not be done. The mere merchants were anxious that the calfskin licence should not be impaired, because of the cost of obtaining it and also because of the yearly stipend they were bound to pay Peter Newall.[1]

This statement was appended to a letter sent to Walsingham by the mere merchants on 1 May 1589. The mere merchants told Walsingham that they had appeared before the mayor and his brethren the previous day and had asked them to convene a council meeting to decide whether or not the mere merchants should be allowed to retail. The mayor and aldermen refused to do so and insisted that the mere merchants should give their opinions first which, to avoid any further dispute, they had agreed to do. It was feared by the mere merchants that the mayor, having their reply in writing, would neither call a meeting nor agree to anything, but seek to prejudice Walsingham against them. Walsingham's help was sought by the mere merchants, but they said that they did not know what the retailers thought about the new proposals. It was alleged also that the opponents of the mere merchants were still denouncing Peter Newall who, the mere merchants alleged, had never been appointed by the city; but, as was mentioned above, this does not seem to have been the case.[2] Despite the remarks made to Walsingham by the mere merchants, a council meeting was held on 2 May 1589 at which Walsingham's letter and the opinions of the London merchants were read out. The council appointed a committee of twelve to consider these matters and decide what answer should be made. It was also agreed that Thurston Hollinshed, gentleman, should go to London to join David Lloyd and help to propagate the city's cause.[3]

The mayor and his associates sent their answer to Walsingham in a letter, dated 7 May 1589, which was read at the council meeting held on that day. This letter pointed out that the London committee was wrong in thinking that the only dispute was between the mere merchants and the merchant retailers; in fact the principal quarrel

---

[1]P.R.O. S.P.D. 12/224/4 I, Chester R.O. M/L/5/253. The latter manuscript was signed William Massey deputy, Richard Rathbone the elder and younger, William Aldersey, Thomas Tetlow, Foulk Aldersey and Richard Knee assistants.
[2]P.R.O. S.P.D. 12/224/4.
[3]Chester R.O. A/B/1/f.220v–221.

of the council and citizens of Chester was with Peter Newall. The mayor told Walsingham that it had been necessary to build a new haven at Chester, and that the levies on the city for this project and the losses sustained by the merchants had helped to impoverish the city, whereby the new haven had not been completed. Therefore, Peter Newall, on behalf of the city, had made many approaches to the privy council and, among other things, had asked for a licence to export calfskins. But, despite receiving more than £36 from the city and contrary to his oath and promise, he had procured for himself a licence to export 2,000 dickers of calfskins, and it was alleged that he had sold this licence to a Bristol merchant for 1,000 marks or more. The mayor also mentioned that Newall had obtained another licence for the benefit of the Chester members of the Spanish Company. It was this deceit that the mayor and his associates wanted to reverse. In its place they hoped to procure a licence which would allow all the Chester citizens to export calfskins. The mayor and council also told Walsingham what they thought about the opinion of the London merchants. They said that the mere merchants had asked for some things which if granted would be a breach of the oaths and usages of the city. This probably refers to the desire of the mere merchants to retail in a trade to which they had not been apprenticed. It was also hoped that an order would be laid down that would allow not only the mere merchants and merchant retailers but also handicraftsmen and all others who were free of the city to engage in overseas trade, as had previously been the custom. This was a much looser interpretation of the matters at issue than that given either by the London merchants or by the mere merchants. In all, forty eight signatures were added at the end of this long and detailed letter.[1]

The mayor of Chester seems to have been determined to leave no stone unturned in his attempt to bring the dispute with the mere merchants to a successful conclusion. On 7 May 1589, as well as writing to Walsingham, he wrote to a friend and native of the city and to an unnamed member of the privy council to canvass support. To the privy councillor the mayor again related the complaint against the mere merchants and especially against Peter Newall. In the other letter he thanked the native of Chester for his previous goodwill towards the city and hoped that he would continue his attempts to bring the controversies to an end. Similarly on 26 May 1589 the mayor wrote to a person to whom the dispute had been

---

[1]P.R.O. S.P.D. 12/224/18. Chester R.O. M/L/5/257–61 for a rough draft of the letter. A/B/1/f221.

referred by the privy council. This letter, very similar to that sent to Walsingham nearly three weeks earlier, asked for the help of this person. The mayor added that he knew of the continual help and goodness that this person had shown to the council and whole city of Chester.[1]

On 9 June 1589 the mayor again wrote to Walsingham in reply to a letter that had reached Chester the previous day. Walsingham's letter contained some directions which he wished the mayor and council to obey. The mayor said that they would abide by Walsingham's orders, "albeit these Articles are far otherwise then to the expectacon of the greatter nomber of the members of this Citie".[2] The content of these orders is not known, but it seems likely that it was similar to the final solution of the disputes at Chester laid down a month later.

V—*The solution*

The order, which brought the long dispute to an end, was issued by the privy council on 9 July 1589.[3] Firstly it was laid down that those who were "meare Merchauntes . . . for the trade of Spaine and Portugall" should be allowed to retail in one trade, but the use of a manual craft was forbidden and the mere merchants were not to be allowed to change from one trade to another once they had made their choice. On the other hand, it was stipulated that all retailers, and not only those who had been merchants previously, should be allowed to trade overseas and retail at the same time and they were also to be allowed to benefit from the licence to export calfskins. It can be seen that in these matters a compromise had been reached for the mayor and council had hoped that all freemen of Chester would be allowed to trade, whereas the mere merchants had wanted to restrict the privilege of trading to those retailers who had been traders in the past. It was also stated that all bearers of public office in Chester could join the "Company of Marchauntes adventurers within the same Citie" and benefit from the calfskin licence, providing they gave up all manual occupations. All free citizens, who were not merchants but retailers or artificers, who were admitted to the company of merchants were to pay a fine of at least £5 to the mayor. These entry fines were to be used for the upkeep of the haven or for any other public use suggested by the

---

[1] *Ibid.*, M/L/5/254, 255–6, 262–4.

[2] *Ibid.*, 90.

[3] *Ibid.*, A/B/1/f. 223 r & v; Morris, pp. 467–8; B. M. Harl MSS. 2104 f304 r & v.

mayor and aldermen. This last provision would obviously be a stumbling block to the entry of small retailers into the merchant company. It is clear that the privy council expected all who wanted to trade to join the Chester merchant company, that is, the company established in 1554 by Queen Mary and not the Spanish Company. Also those merchants who wanted to retail were expected to join the respective gild, for the privy council ordered that "as well the Marchaunte as the retaylor haveing benefit of bothe freedoms which they shall take unto, shall further contribute in all maner of charges to boeth the said Compenies". It was also hoped that trading would be conducted at Chester in a peaceful manner and that the merchants and retailers would "mutuallie trade together by freightinge and shippinge there goode together in ones or moe bottoms as occasion hereafter shalbe offered."

The last direct order to the citizens of Chester concerned the status of the two merchant companies involved in the dispute. This section, which is worth quoting in detail, said that

> "the Marchaunt adventurers of the said Citie shall and maie have and enjoy the benefite of a graunte made unto them by Queene Marie and which by order of this Councell in tyme of former controversie betwene the Marchauntes of London tradinge Spaine and Portingall and the said merchaunte adventurers of the said Citie of Chester in anno 1581 was certefyed by the nowe L. Cheefe Justice of England and the master of the Rooles to be good in lawe, and to which graunte moste of the now merchauntes within the said Citie are sworne".

This order obviously broke the power of the Spanish Company at Chester. Finally it was stated that a copy of the order was to be sent to the customs officials at Chester who were to allow all persons included in the privy council's order to ship calfskins overseas. A copy of the letter written to these officials, on 10 July 1589, has been preserved in the Acts of the Privy Council, following which there is a detailed account of the order laid down the previous day which has been examined above.[1]

The order of the privy council "was openly Red and well thought of" by the Chester council which met on 29 July. Thurston Hollinshed, who had travelled to London during the dispute, told this assembly what expenses he had incurred and it was arranged that two aldermen should audit his account.[2] Nearly eighteen months

---

[1] *A.P.C.* XVII, pp. 371–4.
[2] Chester R.O. A/B/1/f222.

later the auditors informed the Chester council that the expenses of Hollinshed and his fellow petitioners amounted to £60 13s. 4d.[1]

VI—*Postscript*

Despite the large amount of time, effort and money expended by both sides in this long drawn-out dispute the order laid down by the privy council was of little practical importance. The crushing of the Spanish Company's power at Chester came too late, for, as we have seen, there was little direct trade between Chester and Spanish territories after 1585. In addition, only a few of the merchant retailers were able to make good their desire to trade with either Spain or other areas of the continent; Chester's trade with the continent was becoming concentrated in fewer hands and only a handful of merchant retailers were represented. David Lloyd was one of the fortunate few and emerged as one of the most important merchants in the early 1590s. However, he had been quite active during the 1580s and in 1582–3 he was actually engaged in the Spanish trade. Lloyd was probably trading under the authority of the privy council's letter of September 1581 which had temporarily thrown open the Spanish trade.[2] Thomas Linial, another of the retailers' faction, also traded with Spain in 1582–3 and it is clear that the local branch of the Spanish Company did not attempt to control the trade with France; throughout the 1580s David Lloyd, Thomas Linial and other members of the merchant retailers' party were engaged in this trade.

It also seems that the mere merchant ran into difficulties when they attempted to establish retail outlets. In the early part of 1615 a dispute arose between the Company of Mercers and Ironmongers and Thomas Aldersey, a merchant who wished to open an ironmonger's shop.[3] The company tried to stop Aldersey from opening his shop and they received support from the majority of the council. Aldersey's opponents agreed that an order had been set down in 1589 to allow mere merchants to retail in one trade but added that previously this order "was never yet putt in practise".[4] It was alleged that no record could be found to suggest that a

---

[1]*Ibid.*, f. 233v. Individual expenses were £14 3s. 4d. for Richard Bavand, £12 10s. for David Lloyd and £30 for Thurston Hollinshed. The sum of these expenses is less than the recorded total.

[2]See above pp. 83–4

[3]Groombridge, *op. cit.*, p. 78.

[4]B. M. Harl MSS. 1996 fos. 707–8.

merchant had become a retailer under this order, nor indeed had it been suggested until the present mayor "in the behalf of his owne some nowe stirres the question".[1] The privy council gave its ruling on this case on 30 June 1616. At the root of the trouble was the attempt, made by the mere merchants in the earlier part of James I's reign, to exclude the retailers from the benefit of the licence to export calfskins. In retaliation the retailers were determined to deny the mere merchants the benefits of retail trading. Once again the privy council ordered that the mere merchants should be allowed to retail and that the retailers should participate in the licence to export calfskins.

The original cause of the dispute which raged in the commercial community of Chester between 1577 and 1589 was the establishment of the Spanish Company and the attempt made by the Chester members to restrict participation in the trade with Spanish territory. But most of the Chester merchants lost interest in the company in the succeeding decade and a half; when a new charter was granted to the Spanish Company in 1605 only four Chester merchants—Foulk Aldersey, William Aldersey, William Johnson and George Boys—were listed among the large number of members.[2] The new charter again laid down that all retailers and craftsmen should be excluded from the trade but this time the cry of the Chester and Liverpool retailers was taken up all over England, and especially in the west country, and, despite a solid defence by the company, the trade was thrown open to all English subjects in 1606.[3]

Finally it is necessary to examine briefly the steps which were taken towards the end of the period to renew the calfskin licence. On 8 August 1598 the mayor asked Burghley to renew the licence because the merchants had not exported their full quota of skins; it appears that they had exported only some 2,906 dickers of calfskins.[4] This petition brought quick results for on 11 September 1598 the Queen granted authority to the "maior and Cittizens of the saide Cittie of Chester and their Successors for the onelie use benefitt and

---

[1]Thomas Aldersey was the illegitimate son of William Aldersey the elder who was mayor of Chester in 1614–15. Groombridge, *op. cit.*, p. 78.

[2]P.R.O. Patent Rolls, 3 James I, part 6 mem. 10–23. The two Alderseys were also appointed as two of the 61 assistants of the company.

[3]Shillington and Chapman, *op. cit.*, pp. 162–5. Merchants from 15 of the outports were represented in the 1605 charter, but not from Liverpool. However, three Liverpool merchants and no Chester merchants were mentioned in the charter granted to the French Company later in James's reign. C. T. Carr, *Select Charters of Trading Companies, 1530–1707*, Selden Society, 28 (1913), pp. 62–78.

[4]*H.M.C. Salisbury*, VIII, p. 298; IX, pp. 424–5.

behoofe of the merchantes beinge and that shalbe free Citizens
. . . within the space of Nyne yeares" to export the remaining
calfskins. On this occasion there was no mention of the Spanish
Company; rather the mayor was given the power to fine and
imprison those infringing the licence.[1]

---

[1]P.R.O. Patent Rolls, 40 Elizabeth I, part 16, mem. 19–24. David Lloyd once
again had represented the city in this matter. *H.M.C., Salisbury*, VIII, p. 405.

6

THE CHESTER MERCHANTS

THE data relating to the Chester merchants which can be drawn from wills, probate inventories and other sources are rather fragmentary and it is rarely possible to build up a full picture of an individual merchant's activities. Nevertheless sufficient material exists to enable us to say that for many, and especially for the richer merchants, the pursuit of overseas trade was not their only business activity. It is also possible to indicate the level of wealth which the most successful merchants could hope to attain; a level which was substantially lower than that reached by the merchant princes of London and leading merchants of the more prosperous provincial ports. Finally some data are available relating to the position of the merchants within the governing class of the city and also relating to the training and prospects of the younger merchants.

As was shown earlier the foreign trade of Chester was dominated by a small group of important merchants and prominent among these were various members of the Aldersey family; during Elizabeth's reign six of the Alderseys—Foulk, John, Thomas and three Williams—traded with the continent. The first William Aldersey was mayor of Chester in 1560–1, first master of the Chester merchant company of 1554 and died in 1577.[1] John, Thomas and Foulk Aldersey were all sons of the first William and died in 1605, 1607 and 1609 respectively.[2] Foulk Aldersey served as mayor in 1594–5 and John Aldersey in 1603–4.[3] The second William Aldersey was the son of Ralph Aldersey of Chester who died in 1555. He was born in 1543, was twice mayor of Chester in 1595–6 and 1614–15 and died in 1616.[4] The third William, who began trading with the

---

[1] *F.R.*, p. 35; Gross, *op. cit.*, 2, pp. 360–2; "Pedigrees made at the Visitation of Cheshire, 1613" *ed.* G. J. Armytage and J. P. Rylands, *Record Society of Lancashire and Cheshire*, 58 (1909), p. 9.

[2] Cheshire R.O. W.S. 1605 John Aldersey, 1607 Thomas Aldersey, 1608 Foulk Aldersey. They became freemen of Chester in 1568, 1570 and 1560–1 respectively. *F.R.*, pp. 36, 40, 42.

[3] *F.R.*, pp. 73 & 87.

[4] He became a freeman of Chester in 1568. *F.R.*, pp. 40, 74, 101; Cheshire R.O. E.D.A. 2/1 fos.253v–254 (Will of Ralph Aldersey); B. M. Additional MSS. 39925, fos. 4, 19v., 27v.

continent at the very end of Elizabeth's reign, was the son of John Aldersey. He was mayor of the city in 1613–14 and died in 1625.[1]

As a trading family the Alderseys were unrivalled in Elizabethan Chester and individually they were among the wealthiest of the merchants. At his death in 1555 Ralph Aldersey bequeathed the bulk of his estate to his eldest son Hugh, although William, his second son and our second William Aldersey, was quite amply provided for. He was given a house in Eastgate Street, the lease of a garden and house with a tavern underneath, and an eighth of the goods remaining when all other legacies had been settled.[2] In the tradition of the times it was William, the second son, and not Hugh who entered business and became a merchant. At his death in 1616 William Aldersey was living comfortably in a house of some fourteen rooms, situated near the Northgate, which were furnished with goods valued at over £200. His will records that he also owned some land in the city, a tenement and land at Thingwall, land at Denbigh, and leased a house and land at Picton from Sir William Brereton.[3] More details concerning his property were revealed in an inquiry which was held after his death. He possessed more than twenty properties in Chester and more in Denbigh, Eccleston, Gayton, Heswall and Thingwall. He also possessed 104 acres of land scattered around in Handbridge, in the "Town Field in the parish of St. John the Baptist, Chester", and also in Eccleston, Eaton, Moston, Upton, Hoole and Gayton, and he was heir to 60 acres of land and a messuage at Heswall.[4]

William Aldersey must have retired from trade at some time during the reign of James I for at his death in 1616 he did not possess any wine, iron or other commodity of trade.[5] He was, however, an active farmer. His stock of hay and grain in and around Chester was valued at some £46 while at Picton his hay and grain were valued at £41 and he had "winter corne" growing at Picton

---

[1] Cheshire R.O. W.S. 1605 John Aldersey, 1625 Wm. Aldersey. He became a freeman of the city in 1602–3. *F.R.* pp. 86, 99.

[2] Cheshire R.O. E.D.A. 2/1 fos. 253v—254.

[3] *Ibid.*, W.S. 1616 Wm. Aldersey. It was stated in Ralph Aldersey's will of 1555 that he also leased a farm at Picton from Sir William Brereton which was bequeathed to his son Hugh. This was probably the same farm that William Aldersey later leased. The latter's lease was for life and for 21 years after his death.

[4] "Cheshire Inquisitions Post Mortem 1603—1660", I, ed. R. Stewart-Brown, *Record Society of Lancashire and Cheshire*, 84 (1934), pp. 1–5.

[5] He continued to trade with the continent to the very end of Elizabeth's reign. For details of his estate (and other estates) see Appendix II.

and Moston valued at £3. The livestock at Picton, including cattle, oxen, horses, sheep, pigs and poultry, were valued at £112 and the farmhouse furnishings were valued at over £26. Aldersey fully realised the value of a country residence for he recorded that in August 1604 he went to Picton to escape from the plague—"my next neighbor Willm Allen being dead and his house visited, out of which dyed all save one".[1]

Unfortunately an inventory of Foulk Aldersey's estate has not survived but his will shows that he was also a man of means by provincial standards. He owned property in Chester, some land just outside the city, land at Runcorn and Halton in Cheshire and property and land at Hawarden in Flintshire. It is clear from a statement made shortly after his death that he was farming at least some of the land at Hawarden although, unlike the second William, he had not retired from active trade; his will refers to goods that were "beyond the seas". Bequests in his will which were given a value amounted to more than £300.[2]

John Aldersey, like his brother Foulk, was interested in both overseas trade and farming at his death in 1605; his will refers to a number of pieces of land some of which were "part tilled and sowne" and it also refers to some goods he possessed which were overseas.[3] Under this will his son, our third William Aldersey, was made the main beneficiary while Jane Aldersey, William's stepmother, was merely given the goods and property she had brought to John at their marriage.

The wealth of the Chester branch of the Aldersey family became heavily concentrated in the hands of the third William for he was also the heir of his uncle Foulk who died childless. It seems, however, that Foulk Aldersey was rather reluctant to leave his estate to William whom he referred to as "my unkind cosen" whom "I find . . . to be verey geven to be troublesome and Cavelling". It may be, however, that Foulk's judgement was somewhat erratic for he said of his friends "I have found them unkind frends to mee all my lief tyme god forgeve them".[4] But perhaps there was some justification for his harsh references to William. William Aldersey had been appointed as his father's sole executor under the will of 1605 but his administration of the estate was quickly called into

---

[1] B. M. Additional MSS. 39925 f.25 v.

[2] Cheshire R.O. W.S. 1608 Foulk Aldersey; W.C. 1608–9 Foulk Aldersey.

[3] *Ibid.*, W.S. 1605 John Aldersey. He bequeathed £2 to each of his two husbandmen on top of their wages.

[4] *Ibid.*, W.S. 1608 Foulk Aldersey.

question by his stepmother. She claimed that William had helped his father to make his will when he was "sicke of the plague" and not of sound memory and also that he put a fictitious value on a large number of his father's possessions when he drew up an inventory.[1] Whatever the truth of these charges, against which he strongly defended himself, William Aldersey prospered in his career as a merchant. At his death in 1625 his personal estate was valued at over £2,300 and he was owed almost £1,700 which included both good and desperate debts. The major items listed in the inventory of his possessions were over £1,500 in cash, and trade goods—including lead, iron, wine, vinegar, resin and rye— valued at just over £600. Unlike other members of his family he took little interest in agricultural pursuits; his three cows, valued at £8, were no doubt kept to provide fresh milk and perhaps butter for his household.[2]

It has not proved possible to discover a will or inventory for many of the more prominent merchants whereby their wealth and mode of living can be gauged; this is true in the case of such prominent merchants as Thomas Tetlow, William Jewett, Richard Knee and William Massey. Massey was the second son of Richard Massey, who was one of the first wardens of the Chester merchant company of 1554,[3] and received only a small portion of his father's wealth at his death in 1556; Richard, William's elder brother, took the bulk of his father's estate and William had to be satisfied with a legacy of £6 13s. 4d, and a small share of the goods left after all other legacies had been paid.[4] Although neither will nor inventory for William Massey have survived some indication of his way of life can be obtained from the will of his widow, Alice, who established herself in the continental trade after his death.[5] Alice Massey lived in Watergate Street and left the bulk of her estate to Gerard Massey,

---

[1]*Ibid.*, W.C. 1606 John Aldersey.

[2]*Ibid.*, W.S. 1625 Wm. Aldersey. This William is a Jacobean rather than an Elizabethan merchant but details of his estate are given because he began trading with the continent at the very end of our period and also because the family fortunes were in part concentrated in his hands.

[3]Gross, *op. cit.*, 2, pp. 360–2.

[4]Cheshire R.O. E.D.A. 1/2 fos. 211 v–213, W.S. 6/7. Richard Massey mentioned in his will "that presently I have adventure in the *falcon*, in the *george* and in the *Elen*."

[5]"Lancashire and Cheshire Wills and Inventories" part 2, ed. G. J. Piccope, *Chetham Society*, 51 (1860), pp. 227–30. Will dated January 1598, probate date September 1600.

her eldest living son.[1] Her bequests of fourteen gold rings, including the "gold ring with a pearle in it" and "one gold ring with a diamond in it", and fine clothing such as her "best gowne . . . and my velvet hood" or her "grogram gowne with one guard of velvett" or her "best black gowne . . . also my purple gowne" all speak of considerable wealth. To her fourth living son, Lawrence, who became a merchant at the end of Elizabeth's reign, she gave £100 "being his childes part of goodes left unto him by his late father". The Masseys took at least some interest in agriculture for Alice gave to her sister-in-law "one of my kyne called Nann towardes the bringing up her children" and to her servant she gave "my second cowe unbequeathed".

The activities of Edmund Gamull, one of the Chester merchants, and his sons William, also a merchant, and Thomas, the recorder of Chester from 1606 to 1613, are more fully documented than those of William Massey and some of his colleagues.[2] Edmund Gamull traded irregularly with the continent and never featured in the leading group of Chester merchants and he had ceased his trading activities long before his death in 1616 when he was about 79 years old.[3] A probate inventory of his possessions reveals that he lived in a very comfortable fashion owning household goods valued at over £220—of which silver plate accounted for some £123—and possessing over £60 in cash.[4] Edmund Gamull's son, William, who began trading at the end of Elizabeth's reign, seems to have attained greater riches. In a draft will he drew up in 1619 he detailed money bequests totalling more than £2,300 and mentioned property and land he owned in Chester and the surrounding countryside including the six acres "which I lately dyd Inclose being part of Saughall Comen". He also mentioned "the barque that is in partnershipp betwixt" himself and William Aldersey.[5] Part of the land owned by William Gamull had been left to him by his brother Thomas, who died in 1613. Thomas owned a considerable

---

[1]Gerard Massey B. D., Rector of Wigan, was nominated to the Bishopric of Chester but died, in 1616, before consecration. *Ibid.*, p. 227.

[2]J. H. Hanshall, *The History of the County Palatine of Chester* (Chester, 1823), p. 191. Edmund Gamull, described as a gentleman, became a freeman in 1580–1 as did William in 1598—described as son and apprentice of the merchant Edmund Gamull—and Thomas in 1601, described as a gentleman. *F.R.*, pp. 54, 79, 84.

[3]His name does not appear in the 1602–3 port book and the inventory of his possessions made after his death makes no mention of any trade or agricultural goods. Cheshire R.O. W.S. 1617 Edmund Gamull.

[4]*Ibid.*

[5]B. M. Harl. MSS. 1991 fos. 188–199.

amount of land in Cheshire, Staffordshire and Shropshire, the bulk of which—over a thousand acres—was at Buerton in Chester. He also owned the famous Dee Mills which had been leased by his father in 1588, and more property in the city and county of Chester including a salt-works at Middlewich in the tenure of a certain William Eare.[1]

According to the inventory made shortly after his death in August 1603, Richard Bavand, the champion of the merchant retailers, possessed goods valued at around £400.[2] Bavand's house in Chester was extremely well furnished with goods valued at about £300 including a number of pictures, three of which were described as "faire Historicall pictures", and some books—a "Geneva Byble . . . one Cronicle of England and Scotland . . . one Statute Booke", two prayer books and another bible. The inventory also records that Bavand had more than a passing interest in agriculture; his implements, grain and manure in Handbridge and outside the city walls were valued at nearly £80, while behind his house— "In the back"—were two "large swyne" and two "yonge swyne". In the will he made shortly before his death Bavand mentioned that he possessed the manor of Brombrough and land at Brombrough, Bebington and Hargrave.

Wills and probate inventories, although extremely useful to historians, are not without serious limitations. If the inventory of Richard Bavand were taken at its face value it would be assumed that he had retired from business; that this was not so is demonstrated by another manuscript preserved at the Cheshire Record Office. Some of Richard Bavand's friends and acquaintances were questioned after his death about the way his will was drawn up and one of the witnesses declared that "hee heard the decedent give & bequeath unto Michaell Bavand his sonne all such goodes & wares as hee latelie did Committ to his Charge in the voyage wheron hee is nowe gonne behind seas and all the profite of the adventure of the same".[3] A well-known deficiency common to all probate inventories is that they record only the value of moveable possessions and leases and make no reference to real estate, whether it be land or property.

---

[1]"Cheshire Inquisitions Post Mortem", *op. cit.*, II, *Record Society of Lancashire and Cheshire*, 86 (1935), pp. 32–6.

[2]Cheshire R.O. W.S. 1603 Richard Bavand, will and inventory. The inventory consists of three long and narrow sheets which are torn and frayed at top and bottom. The legible entries are valued at nearly £370. The will is also in poor condition.

[3]*Ibid.*, W.C. 1603 Richard Bavand.

Wills often give some indication that property or land was owned but rarely any details; the will of the second William Aldersey, for example, makes only passing reference to his land and property and the same is true of the will of Richard Bavand. Fortunately, however, an inquiry into Bavand's estate was held in 1624 and revealed that at his death in 1603 he owned more than twenty properties in Chester, including seven shops and a "tavern near the High Cross", "divers lands and tenements" across the river in Handbridge and Claverton, a "cottage in the Isle of Mone" and some land at Spital. He also owned the manor of Brombrough and 40 messuages, 40 cottages, 20 tofts, 20 gardens and 560 acres of land in Brombrough, Hargrave and Bebington.[1]

For other prominent Chester merchants only a small amount of information is available but this is of value as it helps us to build up a picture of the provincial merchant's way of life. David Lloyd, the son-in-law of Richard Bavand, was a rich man judging from the thirty or so legacies totalling over £100 which were mentioned in his will. He also mentioned that he farmed some land which he leased and that he had goods "nowe adventured uppon the seas".[2] It seems likely that Thomas Linial, another member of the merchant retailers' party, was engaged in the retail trade as well as in over-seas trade.[3] He owned property in Chester, including eight tene-ments and four shops which he leased out, and he also owned a horse mill at Chester and held a lease of part of the glebe lands belonging to Earlestown rectory.[4] Richard Rathbone, another prominent merchant, lived in Watergate Street and leased a cellar, barn and house in the city. He also owned a field in Huntington and bequeathed a "browne heiffer" to his grand-daughter.[5] Little is known about the first William Aldersey except that he was probably engaged in a little farming on the side for he leased a close of land at Huntington.[6] Similarly, little is known about the activities of Thomas Aldersey who died in 1607 except that he owned "one small Close in Handbridge together with the Corne groweing in the said at the tyme of the deceadentes death".[7]

---

[1]"Cheshire Inquisitions Post Mortem", *op. cit.*, I, pp. 28–31.

[2]B. M. Harl MSS. 1991 fos. 176–9. Dated 12 November 1599.

[3]He was called a mercer when he became a freeman of the city in 1557–8. *F.R.*, p. 33.

[4]Cheshire R.O. W.S. 1603 Thomas Linial, W.C. 1603 Thomas Linial.

[5]*Ibid.*, W. S. 1608 Richard Rathbone.

[6]*Ibid.*, W.C. 1588 William Aldersey.

[7]*Ibid.*, W. S. 1607 Thomas Aldersey.

Most of the merchants who have been discussed so far were rich men by provincial standards and they belonged to the leading group of Chester merchants, but it was possible for such men to be dislodged from their lofty positions and reduced to poverty. John Middleton was one of the more important Chester merchants trading with the continent during the 1560s and he was elected sheriff of the city in 1570.[1] He appears in the customs accounts for the last time in 1572–3 and then seems to have fallen on hard times. By December 1587 Middleton seems to have been close to ruin; stressing his great decay and the need to support his wife and children he asked the city council for a loan of £4 for twelve months.[2] It is obvious that he was in great financial difficulty for in both 1588 and 1592 he asked for the loan to be extended for a further year.[3] The council was willing to help this former sheriff of the city and in 1595 ordered that he should have the benefit of keeping the New Shambles.[4] Three years later the council was concerned about the lack of progress shown by the New Haven project and appointed Middleton as an overseer of that work; he was to see that the labourers worked well and did not waste time, and his expenses were to be met by the city.[5] Whether or not Middleton's declining fortunes were due to events beyond his control or to his own inept dealing is not clear but his career demonstrates that a relatively prosperous merchant was not guaranteed success throughout his life.

Other men, besides John Middleton, failed to obtain a good living at Chester from overseas trade. Robert Evans, who traded with the continent in the early years of Elizabeth's reign, left goods worth only £42 8s. when he died in 1565; these comprised his household possessions, two cows and "a calffe of year olde". His unfortunate widow discovered that she had to pay debts totalling £71 7s. 8d. but presumably she received some money for debts due to Evans.[6] Another merchant, Ralph Thornton, seems to have done even less well than Evans. Thornton traded with the continent

---

[1] Morris, p. 583. Middleton was described as an ironmonger when he became a freeman in 1555 but he became a member of the Chester merchant company and, when his son Randle became a freeman, in 1605 he was described as a "merchant, late of Chester". *F.R.*, pp. 31 & 89; B. M. Harl MSS. 2054 f. 54; Chester R.O. M/L/5/269.

[2] Chester R.O. A/B/I/f. 215.

[3] *Ibid.*, fos. 219 & 237.

[4] *Ibid.*, f. 244 v.

[5] *Ibid.*, f. 254.

[6] Cheshire R.O. W.C. 1574 Robert Evans.

irregularly between the late 1550s and early 1570s but thereafter lost interest in such activity. This is hardly surprising for at his death in 1585 his total estate comprised household goods valued at only £9 5s. 9d. He was, however, owed debts totalling £83 6s. 5d., but unfortunately these were thought to be desperate.[1] Henry Mainwaring was another small-time merchant who lost interest in overseas trade during the 1570s. When he died in 1610 his total personal estate was valued at just over £50; his only possessions apart from his household goods were two cows which "went for herritts" for some land he leased.[2]

It seems obvious that those merchants who were unsuccessful were forced, through the lack of capital, to stop trading. Rather different, however, were the careers of a few men who traded with the continent for a short period and then retired to become successful in a different occupation. Typical of this group was William Dodd who was called a merchant when he became a freeman of the city in 1555.[3] He traded with the continent throughout the 1560s but does not appear in the customs accounts thereafter. When he retired from trade, or perhaps even earlier, Dodd established himself as a mercer and at his death, in late 1598 or early 1599, possessed goods valued at over £400 and was owed debts totalling more than £700. His oxen and horses were valued at just over £28 but the greater proportion of his capital was tied up in his mercery business; he possessed a great range of materials of all qualities and other mercery wares valued at £340.[4]

*   *   *

The long trading careers of men such as Foulk Aldersey and William Massey suggest that good profits could be earned in overseas trade, but to ascribe their wealth to this source alone would be a mistake. Some merchants enhanced their fortunes by advantageous marriages while others, like the third William Aldersey, received generous legacies. Many also operated as part-time farmers while some, such as Richard Bavand and David Lloyd, combined retailing with overseas trade. Others were considerable property owners and no doubt augmented their incomes by leasing their property for profit. In addition there were many more outlets for

---

[1] *Ibid.*, W.C. 1585 Ralph Thornton.
[2] *Ibid.*, W.S. 1610 Henry Mainwaring·
[3] *F.R.*, p. 31.
[4] Cheshire R.O. W.S. 46/38.

the spare capital of Elizabethan businessmen who wished to invest in either long-term or short-term projects.

Perhaps the most natural outlet for merchant capital was investment in shipping. When the *Bear Warwick* was lost in 1575 the account of the losses incurred included a claim by "Fulk Aldersey, Rob. Dryhurst, and Bryan Bland for the shipp and ordinaunce".[1] As was mentioned earlier, Thomas Linial owned a ship of 60 tons which he hired out to some unnamed merchants for a voyage to Spain in 1584 and the *Sunday*, lost off the coast of Ireland in 1567, was owned by three Chester merchants and a sailor from the Wirral.[2] William Jewett, one of the leading merchants in the early decades of Elizabeth's reign, was also a shipowner; in 1562 two ships, the *Magdalene* and *William*, were pressed into the Queen's service to carry troops to Ireland and their owners were said to be "William Juet" of Chester and "Thomas Howghe" of Leighton.[3] Jewett's interest in shipowning continued over a few decades; in the early 1560s the *Grace Jewett* plied regularly between Chester and Spain, and William Jewett was usually the only merchant with goods aboard, while in 1580 his ship, the *Trinity*, was licensed to go to Le Havre with ten men despite "the late Generall Restraint".[4] It seems likely that other Chester merchants also owned ships or parts of ships and support for this suggestion comes from the names of two ships which sailed from the city in the 1550s and 1560s. The *Ellen Goodman* frequently arrived in the Dee with cargoes of iron and wine often belonging to Adam Goodman, while the *Ellen Pillyn* probably belonged to one of the Pillens who were trading with the continent in the early part of Elizabeth's reign.

Some of the Chester merchants benefited directly from their trade by owning a tavern and retailing wine. Thus Ralph Aldersey gave to his son the house which he leased "with the taverne underneythe" while in January 1568 the council licensed Adam Goodman, Simon Mountford and others to keep taverns and retail wine.[5] Similarly Foulk Aldersey seems to have been retailing wine at about the same time.[6]

---

[1]Morris, p. 472.

[2]See above p. 47.

[3]P.R.O. S.P.D. 12/41/55 I. It is interesting to note that the *William* and *Magdalene* both arrived at Chester from Spain on 29 May 1566.

[4]*A.P.C.*, XI, p. 430.

[5]Cheshire R.O. E.D.A. 2/1 fos. 253v–4; Chester R.O. A/B/1/f. 118 Both Mountford and Goodman imported wine during the 1560s.

[6]Morris, p. 426.

The possession and operation of mills provided another outlet for merchant capital at Chester. Edmund Gamull leased the famous Dee Mills in 1588[1] which he was still operating in the early years of the seventeenth century. In 1602 a breach was made in the weir which held back the water to operate the mill wheels and Gamull spent over £500 in repairing it, although at the end of that year it was said that more than £100 was still needed to close the breach.[2] All citizens were bound to have their corn ground at the Dee Mills[3] and in 1570 Margaret Bavand, a widow, was sued by William Goodman, and other lessees of the Mills, for grinding corn belonging to some citizens of Chester at her water mill and at the windmill outside the Northgate, which she leased from the Dean and Chapter.[4] Margaret Bavand was probably the mother of Richard Bavand who also controlled a water mill in 1594.[5]

A short-term outlet for the spare funds of the Chester merchants was mentioned in a letter which was written to Burghley in May 1581 which commented on the lack of money available at Chester for the Queen's Irish affairs:

> "The marchuntes of this Cittie are mannye of them at London, and at this tyme of the yere, they have some gayne by deliverringe their monney heare to drovers and receive the same ageine at london."[6]

In the following month it was stated that

> "the drovers by offerre of *more* profitte have disapointed us of the meanes we had to obtaine money of the marchunts."[7]

On other occasions, however, money was loaned readily to the Queen to finance the provisioning of the army in Ireland and the shipment of troops from the Dee and Mersey: in 1567, 1579 and 1600 some unnamed Chester citizens loaned money to the Queen for such purposes.[8] Sometimes, however, the names of the men who had loaned money to the Queen were given. During the first six

---

[1]See above p. 111
[2]B. M. Harl. MSS. 2084 fos. 204–5.
[3]Morris, p. 101.
[4]*Ibid.*, p. 106; B. M. Harl. MSS. 2081 fos. 253–70; 2083 fos. 482–502.
[5]Chester R.O. A/B/1/f. 243.
[6]P.R.O. S.P. Ireland 63/83/33.
[7]*Ibid.*, 63/83/55. My italics.
[8]*A.P.C.* VII, p. 342; XXX, pp. 314–5, 330: S.P.D. 12/42/72 I, 12/132/66.

months of 1581 George Beverley, who was in charge of the shipment
and provision of troops at Chester, received a total of £3,910 from
various sources to cover his expenses; he received £600 out of the
exchequer, £770 from the receivers of the Queen's customs and
revenues and £2,540 from the merchants and citizens of Chester
and Liverpool. Of this, £340 had been loaned by David Lloyd,
£200 by Richard Bavand and £600 by Roger Lea.[1] Similarly, in
1601 Edmund Gamull loaned the Queen £208 10s.[2] Money loaned
to the Queen was "received of the marchauntes heere upon Like
billes of exchaunge" which were made payable at London, but
unfortunately details of the interest, which was paid for such a
service, have not survived.[3] The availability of money for the
Queen's service depended partly on the presence of alternative
outlets and partly on the speed with which repayment was made;
in February 1581 Burghley was told that if repayment were made
"readilie" money would be available but "yf yt prove otherwise
here will be none to be hadd hereafter".[4]

Some of the Chester merchants were not averse to supplementing
their incomes by making rather shady deals. As we have seen, some
merchants were prepared to smuggle leather abroad before the
licence to export calfskins had been received[5] while others incurred
the displeasure of the city council by entering a stranger's goods
under their own names thus freeing the stranger from the local
duties payable at Chester.[6] In April 1568 William Jewett sold five
hogsheads of wine to Sir Thomas Gerrard at £8 a tun which he
failed to deliver. Jewett's wife, speaking for him, said that the wine
had not been delivered because two hogsheads had been taken for
the Queen's provision and the rest had been sold to a certain Robert
Stringer of Derby for £8 10s. a tun. It was alleged that Jewett had
received a letter saying that if Gerrard did not send for the wine
before a certain day it could be sold to someone else. It was ordered
that unless Jewett could produce this letter the original bargain
should stand.[7]

---

[1] P.R.O. S.P.Ireland 63/84/41. See also 63/80/59.

[2] *A.P.C.* XXXII, p. 371. In 1599 the money required by the Queen was raised
under the auspices of the city council which decided to levy the city's inhabitants
and appointed assessors to lay down what each man should pay. Chester R.O.
A/B/1/f. 256; Morris, pp. 475–6.

[3] P.R.O. S.P.Ireland 63/88/6, 80/55. See 80/55 I for a copy of such a bill of exchange.

[4] *Ibid.*, 63/80/55.

[5] See above pp. 62–3

[6] See for example Chester R.O. A/B/I/ fos. 104 r & v, 230, 237.

[7] B. M. Harl. MSS. 2039 f.176.

Merchants, like many other tradesmen and craftsmen, began their careers by becoming apprenticed for a period of not less than seven years.[1] Young men who entered the Chester merchant community were drawn mainly from the city itself and the Cheshire countryside but also from Caernarvon, Flintshire, Anglesey, Shropshire, Cumberland, Yorkshire, Staffordshire, the Isle of Man and Essex.[2] William Jewett, for example, was "a seconnde sonne to Thomas Iwett of Heyton in Bradforde Dale in the Countye of Yorke" while David Lloyd stated in his will that he had been born in Llaneilian in Anglesey.[3] Perhaps the most surprising entry concerning a young merchant was made in 1597 when it was recorded that Thomas Parker, the son of Samuel Parker, a gentleman of Shenfield in Essex, was apprenticed to John Aldersey for eleven years "to learn the art of a merchant venturer and vintner".[4] There is no doubt, however, that the bulk of entries to the profession were local boys, some following their fathers into trade and some being drawn from landed Cheshire families.[5]

Only nine of the nineteen merchant apprentices for whom indentures are extant became freemen of Chester.[6] Perhaps a small part of this wastage was due to the death of one or two of the apprentices while others, perhaps, broke their indentures and ran away. There seems little doubt, however, that some of the apprentices found it impossible to graduate to the ranks of the fully-fledged merchants because of the high expense involved. Many gilds and companies charged high entry fines[7] and, in addition, the city council sometimes extracted a large fee from an aspirant to the freemen's ranks. When Richard Knee became a freeman in 1568 the heavy fine of £40 was demanded from him but at the council

---

[1]Of 19 young men who were apprenticed to Chester merchants during Elizabeth's reign 8 were bound to serve 7 years, 5 to serve 8 years, 1 to serve 9 years, 4 to serve 10 years and 1 to serve 11 years. Chester R.O. M/Ap/B/1/fos. 25–7, 114.

[2]The 19 young men mentioned above came from Chester 3, Cheshire 3, Shropshire 3, one each from Caernarvon, Cumberland, Essex, Staffordshire, the Isle of Man and Flintshire, and the place of origin of 4 was not given.

[3]"The visitation of Cheshire", ed. J. P. Rylands, *Harleian Society Publications*, 93, p. 263; B. M. Harl. MSS. 1991 f. 176.

[4]Chester R.O. M/Ap/B/1/f. 26v.

[5]Ralph Aldersey was the son of Richard Aldersey of Picton while William Massey's father had roots in both Grafton and Chester. "The Visitation of Cheshire", *op. cit.*, pp. 13, 174, 261–2.

[6]This judgement is made by comparing the details given in Chester R.O. M/Ap/B/1/fos. 25–7, 114 against the *F.R.*

[7]See for example the high fines demanded by the Chester leather companies; D. M. Woodward, "The Chester Leather Industry", *op. cit.*, pp. 92–3.

meeting held on 30 August 1568 it was stated that

> "Richard Kne having married a freman's daughter, hath
> honestly behaven hymself for these six yeres past and is not of
> great substaunce soe as if he should paye the fine of £40 his stock
> wold be consumed. Therefore . . . the said Richard Kne . . .
> shall have againe as rebated £35".[1]

Apart from the cost of joining his company and becoming a freeman
of the city, the young merchant had also to gather together some
capital before he could begin trading. Such financial difficulties
help to explain why young merchants were prepared to travel
overseas as factors for the older merchants.

For some young merchants the problem of acquiring sufficient
capital to establish themselves as independent merchants was not
particularly acute. Some were from rich families and could expect
help from this quarter; Lawrence Massey, for example, was left
£100 by his father. Others married into wealthy families. But for
many young men the early years of their business careers must have
been difficult. It was to alleviate such difficulties that various trust
funds were established at Chester towards the end of Elizabeth's
reign to lend money to young men in need. In 1585 £104, accruing
from the liberal grant made by Sir Thomas White to Bristol some
years earlier, was received at Chester. Out of this sum £100 was to
be loaned to four young men, preferably clothiers, for ten years
free of interest. The remaining £4 was to be given to the mayor and
aldermen for their trouble in administering the fund.[2] The citizens
of Chester benefited in a similar way under the wills of Hugh,
Robert and William Offley, all citizens of London. Hugh Offley
gave £200 to the city to be loaned to four young men, two of whom
were to be merchants and two retailers. They were to keep the
money for three years paying interest of three per cent a year.[3]
Robert Offley gave £600 to the city to be loaned to twenty-four
freemen of whom at least twelve should have been apprenticed in
the city.[4] Finally William Offley bequeathed £300 to the city which
was to be loaned to twelve young men, who had been apprenticed
in Chester, for five years.[5]

---

[1]Morris, pp. 445 & 447. Knee became a freeman on the following day. *F.R.*, p. 40.
[2]Groombridge, *op. cit.*, Appendix 2, p. 219.
[3]*Ibid.*, p. 216. Will dated May 1594.
[4]*Ibid.*, pp. 216–7 .Will dated April 1596.
[5]*Ibid.*, p. 217.

A few of the Chester merchants benefited from these bequests.
At a council meeting held on 16 August 1597 it was decided, by
ballot, who should benefit from the money given by Hugh and
Robert Offley; Randle Bavand and Richard Rathbone, junior,
obtained the £100 set aside for merchants.[1] Three men who traded
with Ireland and the Isle of Man benefited under the will of Robert
Offley[2] and one established merchant received help from these
funds; in 1602 Thomas Allerton, who became a freeman of Chester
in 1581–2 and traded with the continent in the following year, was
one of the beneficiaries under the will of Robert Offley.[3]

By contrast with the Offleys most of the Chester merchants were
not very generous although many of them left small legacies to the
poor of Chester or to the council. John Aldersey, for example, gave
£2 10s. each to the church and parish poor of St. Werburg, £2 to the
almshouses in Common Hall Lane and £1 to the poor of two other
Chester parishes.[4] Similarly David Lloyd gave £1 to the poor of St.
Peter's parish, £2 to the poor of Llaneilian and "one silver Bowle
gilt to the value of twentye nobles" to the city.[5] Foulk Aldersey was
by far the most generous of the Chester merchants; he asked his
wife to distribute black gowns to poor men at her discretion, he
gave £10 to the city to buy a double silver salt engraved with the
Aldersey arms and hoped that the recorder, mayor, justices of the
peace and as many sheriffs' peers as the room would hold would be
invited to his funeral dinner. More important, however, was the
£200 he gave to the city to be loaned out to eight young men at
five per cent. The beneficiaries were to be young mere merchants
or, if there were insufficient of these, the money was to go to young
drapers, mercers or ironmongers. The capital was to be repaid after
seven years and the interest of £10 a year was to be used partly for
charitable purposes, £6 to be given to the city's poor and £2 to poor
prisoners, and partly to cover administrative costs, £1 to the clerk
of the Pentice and £1 to the mayor.[6] The money was loaned out
regularly to young merchants during the reigns of James I and

---

[1]Chester R.O. A/B/1/fos. 249v–250. Randle Bavand, described as an ironmonger
and son of Richard Bavand alderman, and Richard Rathbone, described as an
innholder and son of Richard Rathbone alderman, both became freemen of
Chester on 22 April, 1596. *F.R.*, p. 75.

[2]Chester R.O. A/B/1/f. 274 v.

[3]*Ibid.*; *F.R.*, p. 55.

[4]Cheshire R.O. W.S. 1605 John Aldersey.

[5]B. M. Harl. MSS. 1991 fos. 176–9.

[6]Cheshire R.O. W.S. 1608 Foulk Aldersey; Groombridge, *op. cit.*, p. 214.

Charles I although it seems that some of it was appropriated in the early 1630s to pay off a debt of the city and the remaining money was totally appropriated for other purposes during the civil war.[1]

*   *   *

As might be expected the merchants and richer citizens of Chester tended to form a compact social group linked by common interests and marriage. William Massey, for example, first married Alice, the daughter of Thomas and sister of Richard Bavand and married for his second wife another Alice, the daughter of a merchant, Hamnet Johnson. No children of the first marriage survived but the second Alice bore William Massey six sons and one daughter, Jane.[2] Jane Massey's first husband was Peter Newall, one of the leading mere merchants, who died in 1601. When Jane Newall imported some wine from France in that year as her husband's executrix, it was William Johnson, another merchant, who acted as her factor. This business arrangement bore fruit for William Johnson became Jane's second husband.[3] Thomas Bavand was obviously intent on making good matches for his daughters for, besides William Massey, two other merchants, Walter Fox and John Middleton, became his sons-in-law[4] although, as we have seen, the choice of the latter turned out to be rather unfortunate. Like his sisters Richard Bavand linked his name with that of a leading Chester citizen when he married Jane, the daughter of Randle Bamvill who was a draper and mayor of Chester in 1562-3.[5] Richard Bavand's eldest daughter, Alice, married David Lloyd, thus cementing an alliance which was of signal service to the city authorities and retailers in the struggle against the mere merchants.[6] After Lloyd's death she married Thomas Gamull who later became recorder of Chester.[7]

This tendency to marry partners who lived in the city was followed by many of the merchants and leading citizens. Thus

---

[1]Groombridge, *op. cit.*, pp. 53, 65, 102, 115, 138, 145, 148, 180, 214.

[2]"The Visitation of Cheshire", *op. cit.*, p. 262.

[3]Cheshire R.O. W.S. 1607 William Johnson. He died in January 1608 and it is interesting to note that he was said to be the "sonne and heyer of Hugh Johnsonne of Lysborne, in Portingalle." "Cheshire and Lancashire Funeral Certificates, 1600 to 1678", (ed.) J. P. Rylands, *Record Society of Lancashire and Cheshire*, VI (1882), p. 117.

[4]Cheshire R.O. E.D.A. 2/1 fos. 369v-371.

[5]*F.R.*, pp. 37, 43; "The Visitation of Cheshire", *op. cit.*, p. 266.

[6]*Ibid.*, p. 267.

[7]"Cheshire and Lancashire Funeral Certificates", *op. cit.*, p. 13.

Jane, the daughter of Richard Rathbone, married Edward Allen who began to establish himself in the French trade at the end of Elizabeth's reign.[1] Similarly Edmund Gamull's second wife, Elizabeth, was the widow of William Goodman who died in August 1580 during his mayoralty.[2] This marriage followed Goodman's death with rather unseemly haste for in March 1581 the city council decided that Edmund Gamull, referred to as a gentleman, should be enfranchised because he was going to marry Elizabeth Goodman.[3] By his first wife, also called Elizabeth, Gamull had two sons and two daughters, Anne, who married John Brocke, a gentleman from Upton, and Ellen, who married Richard Swynerton of Knutsford, another gentleman.[4] There was also a tendency for the merchants and citizens of Chester to look for their partners in the surrounding Cheshire countryside. Thus in 1578 the second William Aldersey married Mary, the daughter of John Brereton, an esquire of Eccleston.[5] Similarly the second wife of William Jewett was the daughter of Hamnet Hocknell, a gentleman of Duddon.[6] The first wife of Thomas Linial came from Boughton, just outside Chester, and his second wife was the widow of Thomas Bavand of Liverpool.[7]

The leading merchants of Chester were among the wealthiest citizens and played a prominent role in the government of the city by acting as aldermen, sheriffs and mayors; of the forty nine mayors of Elizabethan Chester thirteen can be identified as trading with the continent and the same is true of twenty five of the city's ninety two sheriffs.[8] Compared with the merchant groups in other towns, however, the political influence of the Chester merchants was slight; at Exeter only four of the fifty mayors were chosen from outside the ranks of the merchants, at Norwich the merchants provided thirty four out of forty seven mayors, while at Bristol

---

[1]Cheshire R.O. W.S. 1608 Richard Rathbone.

[2]"The Visitation of Cheshire", *op. cit.*, p. 269.

[3]Chester R.O. A/B/1/f. 180.

[4]"The Visitation of Cheshire", *op. cit.*, p. 269.

[5]B. M. Additional MSS. 39925 f. 21.

[6]"The Visitation of Cheshire", *op. cit.*, p. 264.

[7]*Ibid.*, p. 271.

[8]Many of the more important merchants became mayor—Richard Bavand who was mayor twice, Foulk Aldersey, William Jewett, the first and second William Alderseys (the latter being mayor again in James I's reign), David Lloyd, Richard Rathbone and William Massey. Other leading merchants who became sheriff but not mayor of Chester were Richard Knee, Peter Newall, Simon and David Mountford.

merchants "usually held the key positions of mayor, chamberlain and sheriffs".[1]

Similarly at both Exeter and Bristol the members of Parliament were frequently chosen from the ranks of the merchants.[2] Only once during Elizabeth's reign, however, did a Chester merchant become member for the city; in 1584–5 Richard Bavand was elected along with Richard Birkenhead, the recorder of Chester from 1575 to 1601. The Earl of Leicester had suggested that a certain Peter Warburton should be chosen to represent the city but as Morris has said, "the citizens were stout enough to make their own choice".[3] Nevertheless, Warburton was chosen as member for Chester for later Parliaments in Elizabeth's reign.[4] Bavand's election in 1584 was probably due to the support he would receive as champion of the city and retailers against the mere merchants; indeed the second William Aldersey, a leading mere merchant and sheriff of the city for 1584–5, was said to have "furthered to the utter moste" the campaign to elect Warburton but the "greater voice chose Mr. Ric. Birkenhed and Mr. Ric. Bavand".[5] It is interesting to note that in an election held during the 1580s Warburton and Birkenhead were chosen from six candidates; Mr. Bavand received only ten votes and Mr. Linial, another merchant, received only one vote, presumably cast by himself.[6]

Although the Chester merchants played an important role in the economic life of the city they did not exercise the same political control as did the merchants of larger provincial ports such as Bristol and Exeter. It was due to this lack of control that the Chester merchants lost the battle which broke out after the establishment of the Spanish Company in 1577 and became intensified after the granting of the calfskin licence in 1584. Had the merchants dominated the council as did their counterparts in Bristol and Exeter the opposition would have found scant opportunity to voice its complaints; such opposition could not have developed at Exeter where,

---

[1]W. G. Hoskins, "The Elizabethan Merchants of Exeter," *Elizabethan Government and Society, Essays Presented to Sir John Neale*, ed. S. T. Bindoff et al. (1961), p. 165; P. McGrath, "Merchants and Merchandise in Seventeenth-Century Bristol", *op. cit.*, pp. xxv–vi.

[2]Hoskins, *op. cit.*, p. 165; McGrath, *op. cit.*, p. xxvi.

[3]J. H. Hanshall, *History of the County Palatine of Chester*, pp. 191–2; Morris, p. 191.

[4]Hanshall, *op. cit.*, p. 192.

[5]Morris, p. 191.

[6]Hanshall, *op. cit.*, p. 192. Hanshall gives 1568 as the date of this contest but it should be dated 1586 or 1589 for only in the parliaments held in those years did Warburton and Birkenhead represent the city together.

in 1558, twenty three of the twenty four members of the Chamber, the governing body of the city, were merchants.[1]

The Chester merchants were also individually less wealthy than the merchants in larger provincial ports. At Exeter the average personal estate of a merchant was valued at about £1,900 gross and this compares very closely with the average personal estate of the Bristol merchants. The inventories of twenty seven Exeter merchants reveal that thirteen of them had gross personal estates valued at over £2,000 and that seven of these were valued at over £3,000.[2] At London, of course, merchants were even richer with personal estates valued on average at nearly £8,000.[3] The restricted nature of Chester's trade failed to produce a sizeable and highly influential group of wealthy merchants such as existed at Bristol and Exeter, and merchant princes were rarely to be seen in any provincial port let alone in a small port like Chester.

---

[1] Hoskins, *op. cit.*, p. 163.

[2] *Ibid.*, p. 172–3.

[3] *Ibid.*, p. 172. Professor Willan has given the case of a London merchant, who died in 1590, whose "estate was found to be worth *only* £828 2*s* 6*d*. when the debts had been paid." T. S. Willan, *Studies in Elizabethan Trade, op. cit.*, p. 212. (The italics are mine.) There were richer merchants than this at Chester but this man would have been among the leading group of merchants.

7

CONCLUSION

A LTHOUGH Chester was the most important trading centre on the west coast north of the Severn it remained one of the smaller provincial ports throughout the sixteenth century. The most important factors restricting trade were the competition of the growing port of Liverpool, with its easier access to the Lancashire textile districts, and the relatively underdeveloped nature of the hinterland, which was also a factor limiting the expansion of Liverpool for much of the sixteenth and seventeenth centuries. Another retarding factor was the gradual silting up of the river, and perhaps the existence of local duties, despite their low level, discouraged some merchants from trading through the city. But the various difficulties facing the Chester merchants did not prevent an expansion of the city's trade. During the first few decades of the century the trade with France and Spain underwent a considerable expansion and the level of wine and iron imports achieved in the 1540s and 1550s was approximately maintained for the rest of the century. Growth in the Irish trade was modest during the first half of the century and fast during the second half. All indicators suggest that, taken as a whole (that is, discounting difficult periods like the 1570s), the sixteenth century was a period of modest prosperity for the mercantile community of Chester.

Compared with developments taking place in the trading patterns of other ports, and especially of London, developments in the trade of Chester appear undramatic. At a time when English merchants were forcing their way into new markets, such as Russia, Persia or Morocco, or redeveloping old and decayed trades, such as those with the Mediterranean and Baltic,[1] the Chester merchants were content to concentrate almost the whole of their energies on the maintenance of their trading connection with France and Spain.

---

[1] T. S. Willan, *The Early History of the Russia Company, 1553–1603* (Manchester, 1956), and *Studies in Elizabethan Foreign Trade* (Manchester, 1959), Ch. 4; R. Davis, "England and the Mediterranean, 1570–1670" in *Essays in the Economic and Social History of Tudor and Stuart England*, ed. F. J. Fisher (Cambridge, 1961), pp. 117–137. R. W. K. Hinton, *The Eastland Trade and the Common Weal in the Seventeenth Century* (Cambridge, 1959), Ch. 1. For a general discussion of the developments taking place in English trade see R. Davis, *The Rise of the English Shipping Industry* (1962), Ch. 1.

Indeed, a specific proposal to draw the Chester merchants and citizens into one of the many schemes for trans-Atlantic exploration aroused little interest. Early in 1584 Chritopher Carleill, the stepson of Sir Francis Walsingham, wrote to Chester to ask for support for a voyage he hoped to make. Only three Cestrians offered support, amounting to ten guineas, and they included William Massey and Thomas Linial, both of whom said they would adventure £5 so long as nineteen others would do the same. It was decided, therefore, that, because of "the decayed estate of this Cittie", Carleill's request should be turned down and he was asked to accept this "unfayned excuse" of the city.[1] Considering the unprofitability of many such schemes and the fate of Sir Humphrey Gilbert's expedition of the previous year, with which Carleill had been involved in a fund-raising capacity, the Chester merchants exhibited that degree of caution inherent in all good businessmen.

Undramatic as the activities of the Chester merchants may seem, however, they were successful within the compass of their narrow aims; trade with the continent—mainly the export of Manchester cottons and tanned calfskins and the import of French wine and Spanish iron—was maintained despite the real difficulties of the 1570s and the problems caused by the Anglo-Spanish war after 1585. In this the Chester merchants did better than the Liverpool merchants who failed to maintain their trade with the continent during the war period. In the Irish trade, however, Liverpool did rather better and developed as a much more important centre than Chester for the import of raw materials, especially linen yarn, and it was this connection with the expanding Lancashire textile industries which was to prove one of the pillars of Liverpool's growth in subsequent generations. Chester, on the other hand, remained far more important both with respect to the quantity and the diversity of commodities exported to Ireland. This partially complementary nature of the trade conducted with Ireland through the ports of Chester and Liverpool was one of the interesting developments taking place in the economy of the north west during the sixteenth century.

The historian is always wise to eschew the pitfalls of debate based on partisan feeling but it seems necessary at this stage to point out that Chester remained a more important trading centre than Liverpool throughout the sixteenth century. Parkinson, the highly partisan historian of Liverpool, accepts that in Elizabeth's reign

[1] E. Rideout, "A Pretended Voyage to America", *Transactions of the Historic Society of Lancashire & Cheshire*, 81 (1930), pp. 54–61; Chester R.O. A/B/1/f. 193v.

"Liverpool had already passed Chester, with its other ports (that is, Conway and Beaumaris), in point of commerce, although it was still greatly inferior to that venerable city in point of wealth, reputation, and dignity",[1] and even the historian of Chester's trade in the late medieval period believes that during "the second half of the sixteenth century Liverpool ousted Chester from her superior position".[2] Liverpool, however, surpassed Chester only in the supply of raw materials for the textile industries of Lancashire and some-times in the supply of skins and hides for workers in the English leather industry. In the other trades—in the export of a wide range of commodities to Ireland and in the shipment of goods to and from the continent—Chester was considerably more important, and in some years, before the war of 1585 when Liverpool's continental trade ceased altogether, Chester merchants were exercising a sig-nificant measure of control over the continental trade of Liverpool. If we are looking for the emergence of Liverpool as the premier port of the north west we must look outside the sixteenth century and most likely to the period after the interregnum.[3]

It has been suggested also that in the 1560s "London held a monopoly of commercial activity while every other port in the kingdom, with the possible exception of Bristol, appears to have been in an advanced state of decay" and also that "London maintained the supremacy over the outports that it had already won in 1559, while Newcastle, Hull, Boston, King's Lynn, Portsmouth, Southampton, Poole, Weymouth, Bristol and Chester remained

---

[1] C. N. Parkinson, *The Rise of the Port of Liverpool* (Liverpool, 1952), p. 29. This statement is based on the customs collected in the Port of Chester during 1586—this source misrepresents the true position for it does not take into account the French wine imported at Chester on which duty was not paid. The great bulk of the duty collected at Liverpool was paid on linen yarn imported from Ireland which carried a relatively high duty. Parkinson relied heavily on secondary and printed primary sources and did not use the port books to analyse the trade of Liverpool and Chester.

[2] Wilson I, p. 170, note 5. Wilson does not give any evidence to support this state-ment.

[3] The author intends to look more fully at the rivalry between Chester and Liver-pool to try to set the record straight. It seems unlikely that Liverpool ousted Chester under the early Stuarts for in that period, and especially in the reign of Charles I, Chester's trade underwent a massive expansion based on the import of livestock on the hoof from Ireland. By 1638–9 approximately 18,000 animals (mainly cattle) were being shipped into the Dee. In Elizabeth's reign less than 100 ships entered the Dee each year but in 1638–9 some 470 ships entered the Dee carrying livestock as well as the ships engaged in other trades. P.R.O. E190/1336/3.

'manifestly decayed' ".[1] Such generalisations may comfort those historians who speculate about the course of English trade solely on the basis of data abstracted from the London port books, but detailed studies of some of the ports mentioned above suggest that decay was not endemic. Professor Davis has shown that the "last four decades of the sixteenth century . . . saw a continuous and rapid growth of Hull's overseas trade" while the "East Anglian ports in the later sixteenth century were centres of prosperity, driving a thriving coastal and foreign trade, and making a substantial contribution to the wealth of England".[2] At the same time the Tyne was a centre of great activity; the amount of coal shipped out of the Tyne increased from nearly 33,000 tons in 1563–4 to nearly 240,000 tons in 1608–9.[3] Similarly the historian of Elizabethan Exeter, although not entering into a detailed analysis of the port's trade, talks of the "bustling commerce" of the city.[4] Thus it is evident that many of the outports, including the major ports of the north west, were not "manifestly decayed" during the second half of the sixteenth century. It seems likely that some historians have been misled by the rather melodramatic petitions emanating from the merchant groups in the outports; those merchants, seeking some privilege or other from the crown, fought to gain the ear of the Queen or privy council and in so doing over-represented their difficulties. Important though the trade of London was throughout the later sixteenth century it is clear that insufficient attention has been paid to the outports some of which, at least, were showing real signs of development and growth during the period.

Although severe criticisms have been levelled against the port books as sources of historical data[5] they have allowed historians to write accounts about the trade between England and other countries and also about the trade of individual ports. By using data abstracted from the port books much can be said about the commodities and the directions of trade, about the regularity and the approximate volume of trade, and about a whole range of related

---

[1]L. Stone, 'Elizabethan Overseas Trade', *Economic History Review*, Second Series, 2 (1949), pp. 39 & 50. Stone provided very little evidence to support his generalisations about the outports.

[2]R. Davis, 'The Trade and Shipping of Hull 1500–1700', *East Yorkshire Local History Series*, No. 17 (1964), p. 10; N. J. Williams, 'The Maritime Trade of the East Anglian Ports, 1550–1590', Unpublished D. Phil. Thesis (Oxford University, 1952), p. 310. See also pp. iii & 300–10 where he forcibly makes the point that the role of the outports has been seriously underestimated.

[3]J. U. Nef, *The Rise of the British Coal Industry* (1932), 2, Appendix D.

[4]W. T. MacCaffrey, *Exeter, 1540–1640* (Cambridge, Mass. 1958), p. 165.

[5]For a discussion of the Chester port books see Appendix III (ii).

questions. The port books are also invaluable in providing us with an index of merchants and an account of their trading activities. To this basic list of merchants much more information can be added both about their activities as a commercial group and also about their activities as individuals. But despite the wealth of information which exists about some aspects of the merchant's way of life in other respects he remains a rather shadowy figure. It has proved impossible to discover any intimate details about the ways in which the Chester merchants organised their businesses;[1] it is not possible to say either what kind of profit they could hope to make from trade or the extent to which their by-occupations, and especially their interest in agriculture and landed estates, were geared to profit-making or the generation of social prestige. As with many pieces of detailed research the number of questions which must remain unanswered equal or surpass the number which it has been possible to answer.

The study of a small port, like Chester, is unlikely to throw up questions of major controversy but such studies do help to expand our knowledge of the economy and the workings of local society. To the national economy it mattered little whether the smaller ports, like Chester and Liverpool, prospered although, within the local economies they served, such ports played a crucial role. For the better-off classes of the region the import of wine and other luxuries brought a higher standard of living, while many other imports—such as iron, wool, linen yarn and skins—were indispensable to the maintenance of local industry. The export trade, on the other hand, provided an outlet for industrial produce and both branches of trade brought employment for workers in the tertiary sector, such as merchants, shopkeepers, carriers, porters, boatmen and sailors. Finally, it is worth reflecting that the greatest upheaval in the life of modern Britain, the Industrial Revolution, was initially a development which took place within relatively narrow geographical bounds—a development which scarred the landscapes of the north west and midlands more than those of other regions—and it was this area which was served by the ports of Chester and Liverpool. The trade passing through Chester did much to facilitate the early development of this region although as the pace of change gathered speed in the later seventeenth century it was Liverpool, with easier access to the Lancashire textile districts, which emerged as the major port of the north west.

---

[1]Unfortunately it has not proved possible to locate any ledgers or letter books belonging to the Chester merchants.

APPENDIX I. *Details of the Trade and Shipping of Chester.*

(A) *The Import of Wine and Iron from France, Spain and Ireland*[1]

(A.=E.190; B.=E.122; C.=S.C.E; for further details see Appendix III.)

		Wine (tuns)	Iron (tons)
1558–9	(C)	138	273
1559–60	(C)	135	336
1562–3	(B)	157	363
1564–5	(C)	311	202
1565–6	(A)	53	122
	(C)	42	168
1568–9	(C)	140	102
1570–1	(C)	173	82
1572–3	(C)	63	184
1576–7	(A)	127	158
	(C)	101	54
1577–8	(C)	128	185
1578–9	(C)	260	68
1579–80	(B)	173	139
	(C)	134	152
1580–1	(C)	200	125
1581–2	(C)	139	46
1582–3	(A)[2]	406	99
	(A)[3]	485	99
	(C)	396	22
1583–4	(C)	414	93
1584–5	(A)	538	28
	(C)	442	44
1585–6	(B)[4]	—	188
	(C)	306	49
1587	(B)	—	63
1587–8	(C)	89	33
1588	(B)	—	125
1589	(B)	—	21
1591–2	(C)	353	116
1592–3	(A)	229	100
	(C)	270	60
1602–3	(A)	219	42

Notes;

[1]Small amounts of iron which were shipped to Chester along the coast have been excluded although it is sometimes difficult to establish the ports of origin in the Sheriffs' Customs Entry Books. This may have inflated the data derived from this source to a small extent. Much of the iron arriving at Chester along the coast was probably made in England. Data is given to the nearest whole number.

[2]The book of the Controller of Chester.

[3]The book of the Searcher of Chester.

[4]The E122s of the 1580s do not give details of wine imported at Chester.

(B) *Ships Entering and Leaving Chester in the Overseas Trade*

(i) Ships Entering Chester.

From	1565–6	1576–7	1582–3	1584–5	1585	1587	1588	1589	1592–3	1602–3
Ireland	35	78	49	62	46	53	43	44	71	67
Spain	7	6	4	1	—	—	—	—	1	—
France	3	1	9	13	7	3	3	5	7	5
Isle of Man	2	7	8	8	12	7	8	12	9	9
Scotland	—	—	2	1	3	4	2	2	3	9
Baltic	—	—	—	—	2	1	—	—	—	—
Portugal	—	—	—	1	—	—	—	—	—	—
Norway	—	—	—	—	—	—	—	—	—	1
Total	47	92	72	86	70	68	56	63	91	91

(ii) Ships Leaving Chester.

To	1565–66	1576–77	1582–83	1584–85	1585–86	1587	1588	1589	1592–93	1602–03
Ireland	20	65	45	56	80	61	44	52	81	133
Spain	12	} 9	10	2 } +4	—	—	—	—	—	—
France	5	}	3	8 }	8	7	4	4	8	6
Isle of Man	—	5	4	4	9	5	4	6	8	4
Scotland	—	—	2	1	5	5	—	2	2	—
Low Countries	—	1	—	—	1	—	—	—	1	—
Total	37	80	64	75	103	78	52	64	100	143

Note:

The data provided in these tables cannot be used to assess the relative importance of the different trades. In the Irish trade many ships made frequent voyages and most of them carried only a small cargo. In the continental trades, however, the round voyage took much longer but ships tended to be fully laden, especially for the return run to Chester. Also comparison is rendered difficult because of variations in the size of ships occupied in the different trades:—

Average Burthen of Ships (in tons)

	1565–6	1582–3	1592–3	1602–3
Irish trade	16·5	23	19	28·5
Continental trade	38	49	58	61
Manx trade	6	5	10	16

(C) *Ships in the Continental Trades, by Port of Provenance*

(i) Ships Entering Chester

Ships of:–	1565–6	1576–7	1582–3	1584–5	1587	1588	1589	1592–3	1602–3
Chester	5	5	3	5	—	—	1	3	—
England	2	1	7	1	4	2	3	1	—
Spain	2	—	—	—	—	—	—	—	—
France	—	—	1	8	—	—	—	2	3
Wales	—	—	1	1	—	—	—	—	—
Isle of Man	1	—	—	—	—	—	—	—	—
Scotland	—	1	1	—	—	—	1	1	—
Ireland	—	—	—	—	—	1	—	—	—
Low Countries	—	—	—	—	—	—	—	1	3
Total	10	7	13	15	4	3	5	8	6

(ii) Ships Leaving Chester

Ships of:—	1565–6	1576–7	1582–3	1584–5	1587	1588	1589	1592–3	1602–3
Chester	9	7	5	5	—	1	1	3	1
England	3	3	6	2	6	2	2	2	1
Spain	2	—	—	—	—	—	—	—	—
France	—	—	1	7	—	1	—	2	3
Wales	—	—	1	—	—	—	—	—	—
Isle of Man	3	—	—	—	—	—	—	—	—
Scotland	—	—	—	—	1	—	1	1	1
Low Countries	—	—	—	—	—	—	—	1	—
Total	17	10	13	14	7	4	4	9	6

(D) *Ships in the Irish Trade, by Port of Provenance*

(i) Ships Entering Chester

Ships of:–	1565–6	1576–7	1582–3	1584–5	1587	1588	1589	1592–3	1602–3
Chester	2	13	21	28	25	19	7	22	21
River Dee*	31	30	11	15	13	11	11	21	23
Ireland	2	32	13	10	12	11	22	23	14
England	—	3	4	7	3	1	3	4	3
Isle of Man	—	—	—	—	—	—	—	1	1
Scotland	—	—	—	—	—	—	—	—	3
Wales	—	—	—	2	—	1	1	—	2
Total	35	78	49	62	53	43	44	71	67

*Ships said to belong to the villages of the Wirral or to anchorages in the estuary.

(ii) Ships Leaving Chester

Ships of:–	1565–5	1576–7	1582–3	1584–5	1587	1588	1589	1592–3	1602–3
Chester	—	5	20	25	30	19	14	24	33
River Dee	16	34	14	20	17	9	20	30	62
Ireland	4	23	10	9	11	9	16	22	20
England	—	2	—	2	3	6	1	5	4
Isle of Man	—	—	1	—	—	—	—	—	—
Scotland	—	1	—	—	—	1	—	—	5
Wales	—	—	—	—	—	—	1	—	2
Continent	—	—	—	—	—	—	—	—	7
Total	20	65	45	56	61	44	52	81	133

(E) *Ships Entering and Leaving Chester in the Coasting Trade*

(i) Ships Entering Chester:—

From:–	1584–5	1586–7	1592–3	1595 (6 months)	1598 (6 months)	1602–3
Cumberland and Westmorland						
Ravenglass	—	2	—	—	1	—
Parton	—	1	—	—	—	—
Workington	—	1	—	—	—	2
Lancashire						
Liverpool	—	—	19	1	4	—
Alt	—	—	—	1	—	—
Ribble	—	—	—	1	—	—
Wyre	—	—	—	2	—	—
Wales						
Beaumaris	—	—	5	—	2	3
Porthdinlleyn	—	—	—	—	—	1
Fishguard	—	—	—	—	—	2
Milford	—	—	—	—	—	1
Barmouth	—	—	1	—	—	—
South West						
Bristol	—	—	—	—	—	1
Poole	—	—	—	—	1	—
Plymouth	—	—	—	—	—	1
Fowey	—	—	—	—	—	1
Barnstaple	—	—	—	—	—	5
London	1	2	—	1	1	2
Ipswich	—	—	—	—	—	3
Place not given	—	1	—	—	—	—
Total	1	7	25	6	9	22

(ii) Ships Leaving Chester

For:-	1584–5	1586–7	1592–3	1595 (6 months)	1598 (6 months)	1602–3
Cumberland and Westmorland						
Ravenglass	4	5	—	2	—	6
Parton	—	1	—	—	—	—
Workington	—	—	—	5	1	5
Milnthorpe	1	—	—	—	—	3
Cockermouth	1	—	—	—	—	—
Lancashire						
Liverpool	—	—	—	2	1	3
Alt	—	—	—	1	—	—
Preston	—	—	3	2	2	4
Peel	—	—	—	—	—	5
Lancaster	—	—	1	—	1	—
Sankey	—	—	—	—	—	2
Clitheroe	—	—	1	—	—	—
Wyer	—	—	1	—	—	—
Wales						
Beaumaris	1	—	8	6	3	21
Porthdinlleyn	—	—	2	4	1	1
Caernarvon	1	—	5	1	—	4
Conway	—	—	—	—	—	4
Aberdovey	—	—	—	—	—	1
Barmouth	1	—	1	—	—	1
Bangor	—	—	—	—	—	1
Milford	—	1	—	—	—	—
Fishguard	—	—	—	—	—	1
Mostyn	—	—	1	—	—	—
South West						
Plymouth	—	—	—	—	—	2
Fowey	—	—	—	—	—	1
Place not given	—	—	6	—	—	1
Total	9	7	29	23	9	66

APPENDIX II: *Details from the Inventories of Nine Chester Merchants*

		Household goods			Trade goods			Farm goods			Money			Total			Debts He is owed			He owes		
		£	s.	d.	£	s.	d.	£	s.	d.	£	s.	d.	£	s.	d.	£	s.	d.	£	s.	d.
Robert Evans	1565	39	6	8	—			3	1	4	—			42	8	0	n.g.			71	7	8
Ralph Thornton	1585	9	5	9[1]	—			—			—			9	5	9	83	6	5	n.g.		
William Dodd	1598	49	6	8	340	0	0[2]	28	6	4[3]	—			417	13	0	711	16	0	n.g.		
Richard Bavand	1603	289	3	3	—			79	7	6	—			368	10	9[4]	n.g.			n.g.		
Henry Mainwaring	1610	47	5	7	—			4	13	4[5]	—			51	18	11	n.g.			n.g.		
Christopher Challoner	1613	43	11	5	—			—			—			43	11	5	n.g.			n.g.		
Edmund Gamull	1616	227	6	9	—						62	5	0	289	11	9	n.g.			40	11	6
William Aldersey	1616	349	2	3[6]	—			229	18	0[7]	100	0	0	679	0	3	95	0	0	n.g.		
William Aldersey	1625	242	10	9	607	10	2	8	0	0	1529	16	0	2387	16	11	1695	13	10	n.g.		

Sources: Cheshire R.O. W.C. 1565 and 1574 Robert Evans; W.C. 1585 Ralph Thornton; W.S. 46/38; W.S. 1603 Richard Bavand; W.S. 1610 Henry Mainwaring; W.S. 1613 Christopher Challoner; W.S. 1617 Edmund Gamull; W.S. 1616 William Aldersey; W.S. 1625 William Aldersey.

Notes:

1 Including a mare valued at 12s.

2 A very wide range of mercery wares.

3 Oxen and horses.

4 Many entries in this inventory are illegible so that the total will be more than that recorded here.

5 Two 'kyne'.

6 Including the lease of a garden valued at £6 13s. 4d. and a tenement at Picton valued at £100.

7 Including a lease of land valued at £20 13s. 4d.

APPENDIX III: *A Note on the Trade Statistics*

(*i*) List and Description of the Chester Port Books, Customs Accounts, and Sheriffs' Customs Entry Books.

(A) *The Port Books* (P.R.O. Exchequer, K.R. Port Books)

Date	Reference	Officer in Charge of the Book	Comments
1565–6	E190/1323/1, 10	Customer	Two half-year books. Overseas trade only.
1576–7	E190/1324/17	Searcher	Overseas and coasting trades.
1582–3	E190/1325/7	Searcher	Overseas and coasting trades.
	E190/1325/8	Controller	Overseas trade only.
1584–5	E190/1325/15	Searcher	Overseas and coasting trades.
1592–3	E190/1326/6	Surveyor	Overseas trade only. This book does not give details of wine imported.
	E190/1326/15	Searcher	Overseas and coasting trades.
1595	E190/1327/10	Customer and controller	Coasting trade only for the six months Easter to Michaelmas.
1598	E190/1327/20	Customer and controller	Coasting trade only for the six months Easter to Michaelmas.
1600–1	E190/1327/28	Customer	Overseas trade only for the six months Michaelmas to Easter.
1602–3	E190/1328/20	Searcher	Overseas and coasting trades.

The port books run from Michaelmas to Michaelmas except where it is stated otherwise.

(B) *The Customs Accounts* (P.R.O. Exchequer, K.R. Customs Accounts)

Date	Reference	Comments
1562–3	E122/31/5, 200/4	Two books cover the year from Michaelmas to Michaelmas.
1585–6	E122/31/18–20, 22	Four books cover the year from Michaelmas to Michaelmas.
1587	E122/31/24–7	Four books—Xmas to Xmas.
1588	E122/31/28–31	Four books—Xmas to Xmas.
1589	E122/31/32–5	Four books—Xmas to Xmas.
1590	E122/31/36, 37	Two books—Xmas to March and June to September.

(C) *The Sheriffs' Customs Entry Books* (Chester R.O. S.C.E.)

		Years Studied	*Comments*
Vol. 10	1551–9	1558–9	—
Vol. 11	1559–69	1559–60, 1564–5, 1565–6, 1568–9	No entries for 1560–1, 1561–2, 1563–4. Entries for 1562–3 are badly damaged.
Vol. 12	1570–80	1570–1, 1572–3, 1576–7, 1577–8, 1578–9, 1579–80	No entries for 1571–2, 1573–4, 1574–5. Entries for 1575–6 are badly damaged.
Vol. 13	1580–4	Every year	—
Vol. 14	1584–1603	1584–5, 1585–6, 1587–8, 1591–2, 1592–3, 1602–3	No entries for 1586–7, 1588–9 to 1590–1, 1593–4 to 1601–2.

(*ii*) A Note on the Port Books

This study, and especially chapters 2 to 4, has been based mainly on data abstracted from the Chester port books even though such documents have been attacked by some historians as being unreliable and of limited value.[1] The port books, it has been suggested, failed to record the total volume of trade of individual ports or regions because of two kinds of fraudulent activity; smuggling by the merchants, sometimes with the connivance of the customs officials, and the deliberate under-registration of trade by the officials themselves in an attempt to augment their meagre stipends. It has been suggested further that the administration of the customs was probably more efficient in London than in the provincial ports and that the further a port was situated from Westminster the more difficult it was for the government to exercise effective control.[2]

---

[1] See the following critical discussions of the port books—N. J. Williams, "Francis Shaxton and the Elizabethan Port Books", *English Historical Review*, 66 (1951), pp. 387–94; N. Williams, *Contraband Cargoes* (1959), chap. 2; N. Williams, "The London Port Books", *Transactions of the London and Middlesex Archaeological Society*, 18 (1955), pp. 13–26; G. D. Ramsay, *English Overseas Trade During the Centuries of Emergence* (1957), chap. 6. For rather less hostile assessments of the port books see R. W. K. Hinton (ed.) "The Port Books of Boston 1601–1640", *The Lincoln Record Society*, 50 (Hereford, 1956), pp. xxxii–iii; R. C. Jarvis, "Sources for the History of Ports", *Journal of Transport History*, III (Leicester, 1957–8), p. 81; T. S. Willan, *Studies in Elizabethan Foreign Trade* (Manchester, 1959), pp. 65–6. W. B. Stephens, *Seventeenth Century Exeter* (Exeter, 1958), pp. xix–xxvi. The historian of Southampton's trade in the later sixteenth century considers that the Southampton port books were fairly accurate; Wiggs, *op. cit.*, pp. 25–6. See also two recent discussions: W. B. Stephens, "The Exchequer Port Books as a Source for the History of the English Cloth Trade", *Textile History*, i (1969), pp. 206–13; D. M. Woodward, "Short Guides to Records, 22. Port Books", *History*, 55 (1970), pp. 207–10.

[2] Ramsay, *op. cit.*, p. 190; Williams, *Contraband Cargoes*, p. 42; "The London Port Books", *op. cit.*, p. 15 It is interesting to note, however, that Williams wrote of malpractices at London being an "open secret"—*Contraband Cargoes*, p. 33. The thesis that administration of the customs was less lax at London than elsewhere would not seem to be proven. There is little doubt that the efficiency of administration varied between the different ports and in the same port over time.

The impression given by some historians is of widespread smuggling at all ports. It has been pointed out, however, that smuggling "is usually a response either to prohibitions or to high duties" and that, on the whole, duties were not high in Elizabethan England. The official valuation of goods was unchanged between 1558 and 1604 so that fixed, *ad valorem* duties became a smaller percentage of the real value of cargoes as the Elizabethan inflation proceeded.[1] There were, however, some heavy duties; French wine bore a duty of 50s. 4d. a tun, which early in Elizabeth's reign may have amounted to a duty of about 80 per cent *ad valorem*, although considerably less by 1603. Similarly, the duty on exported wool was heavy and leather bore a heavy duty, so far as export was allowed, but the main specific duty on exports, that on cloth, was not high for native merchants. Thus it has been pointed out that "the whole system of duties . . . suggests that . . . smuggling would be highly selective" and that successful wine smuggling, for example, would obviously be a profitable occupation.[2]

At Chester it seems unlikely that there was much smuggling in the continental trade during Elizabeth's reign. In the first half of the period the main export was woollen cloth which bore a low duty, while the main export in the second half of the period was tanned caifskins which bore a nominal duty of 1s. on every 120 skins. Similarly iron, one of the main imports, bore the low duty of 4s. a ton while the Chester merchants were relieved of the duty on French wine, the other main import, in 1567. There was thus little incentive for the would-be smuggler in the continental branch of Chester's trade.

It is possible to make a check on the port books by comparing the details of imported wine and iron given in the port books with the corresponding details provided by the local customs accounts kept by the Chester sheriffs. In the five years for which details are available from both sources—1565–6, 1576–7, 1582–3, 1584–5 and 1592–3—the port books give a higher figure for wine and iron imports in four years.[3] A higher total of iron is given in the sheriffs' book for 1565–6 because it records one more cargo than do the port books and also because the royal official under-recorded the amount of iron in every other cargo by an average of about twenty one per cent. Similarly in 1592–3 the port book gives a slightly lower figure for some of the main wine cargoes of that year, but the bulk of the difference between the totals recorded in the sheriffs' book and the port book is due to a number of small cargoes of wine, which feature only in the sheriffs' book, which

---

[1]T.S. Willan (ed.) *A Tudor Book of Rates* (Manchester, 1961), pp. xliii, xlviii.

[2]*Ibid.*, pp. xiii, xlvii–viii. For example it has been suggested that at Bristol, at the end of Elizabeth's reign, less than half the wine unloaded there was paying duties. Williams, *Contraband Cargoes*, p. 52.

[3]Note that in Appendix I (A) it is recorded that the local book for 1584–5 gives a higher total of imported iron than does the port book. This was because the entries in the port book stopped slightly before the entries in the local book and a cargo of 30 tons of iron, imported in October 1585, was recorded in the latter. During the period covered by both books the port book records the higher total.

probably had been carried along the coast rather than from overseas. A comparison between these two sources would suggest, therefore, that the royal officials were generally more energetic in pursuit of their business than were their local counterparts and that the port books are a more reliable source, on average, than the local books.[1]

Another way to check the veracity of trade statistics obtained from such sources is to see whether or not they mirror what contemporaries thought about the state of trade. Thus to notice that the level of wine and iron imports at Chester seems to have been low during the 1570s, when the merchants suffered heavy losses and complained bitterly about the decayed nature of their trade, suggests that the sources are providing us with a picture which corresponded approximately to the real situation. It is not suggested that the details given in chapter 3 and Appendix I (A) are accurate statistics but that they give a fair indication of the broad trends of Chester's trade with the continent.

It seems likely that in the Irish trade smuggling was more prevalent at times. As we saw earlier, attempts were made in 1575 to curb the fraudulent activities of the Irish merchants and it was alleged, at that time, that one of the Dublin merchants had paid the Chester searcher 20 marks a year to ignore his frauds. The searcher was always the officer most likely to be corrupted because he could defraud the customs without his fellow officers knowing about it; it was the searcher's job to check a ship's cargo before sailing after it had been cleared through the customs.

A report sent to Burghley in January 1584 refers to various aspects of smuggling and other nefarious activities in the Port of Chester. The controller of Chester had informed his London masters that there had been of late years very many " unlawfull conveyances of Lether, corne and other merchandyzes and some disorders used in the Crekes of the same porte of Chester". These abuses, it was thought, were due partly to the negligence of the customs officers, especially the searcher and "Thomes Whixsted" the customer's deputy at Liverpool, and partly to the disobedience of merchants and shipowners. It had also been discovered that "under color of transportacions from porte to porte" and of the Queen's provisions for Ireland

> "great quantyties not onlie of corne, vyctualls, Clothes and other merchandizes have bene unlawfullie shipped and conveied out and from the Crekes and members of the said porte into the Realmes of Spayne, ffraunce, Scotlande, Ireland and other partyes beiond the Seas, but also of plate, brasse, weynscote, tymber, and other wares by her Maiesties lawes prohybyted to be conveied to any the parties beiond the Seas".

---

[1]Williams's disenchantment with port books in general is partly due to his discovery that at Yarmouth the local Water Books recorded a higher level of trade than did the port books. For Southampton, however, the port books were far more detailed than the local books. Williams, "Francis Shaxton", *op. cit.*, p. 388; Wiggs, *op. cit.*, pp. 25–6.

Goods had also been brought from Ireland without any custom being paid.[1] Whether any action was taken is not known but it will be remembered that in 1588 the mayor of Dublin spoke of the overhard dealing of the customer, searcher and other officials at Chester.

The report of 1584 demonstrates that the smuggling of commodities whose export was prohibited was always likely[2] and it also shows that in the early 1580s at least the controller at Chester was not venal. It suggests further that the "creeks" of Chester, including Liverpool, where the enforcement of regulations would be more lax, were more notorious for their smuggling than the head port.[3] The statement that goods had been brought to Chester from Ireland free of duty may help to explain the relatively small quantities of skins, wool and flocks that were recorded in the 1582–3 and 1584–5 port books.[4]

Thus it seems likely that the port books give a fairly accurate picture of Chester's continental trade, although they are probably not so accurate for the Irish trade. While admitting that the port books are not too reliable it must be remembered that without them it would be impossible to discuss the trade of a small provincial port in any meaningful way. The port books, at least, give the minimum volume of trade passing through a particular port and in dealing with the commodities of trade it is only sensible to quote accurately data abstracted from the port books while realising that they are not "statistics".

---

[1]B. M. Lansdowne MSS., 40 f. 46 r & v.

[2]See for example, the smuggling of leather out of the Dee in the early 1580s above pp. 62–3.

[3]Some smuggling took place at Liverpool in this period. See above p. 63.

[4]See above p. 7.

Appendix IV:

Maps showing places mentioned in the text

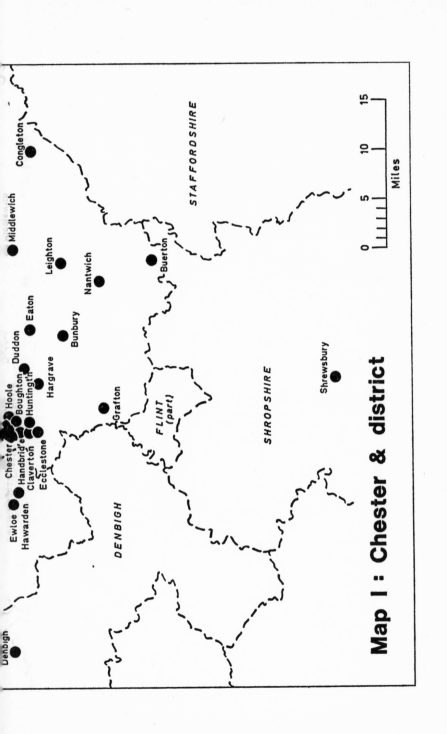

Map I : Chester & district

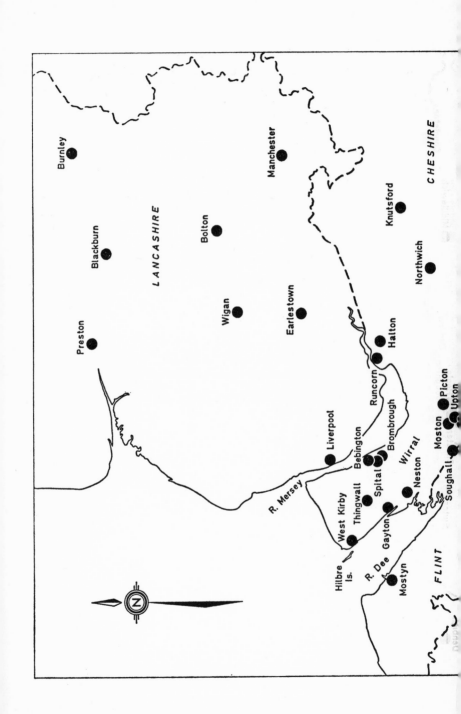

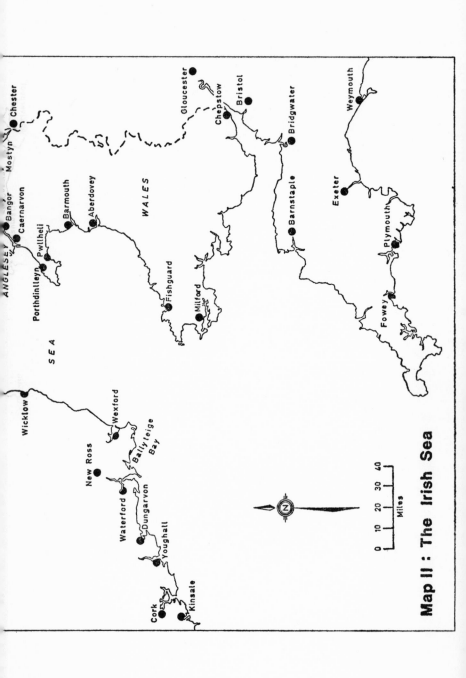

Map II : The Irish Sea

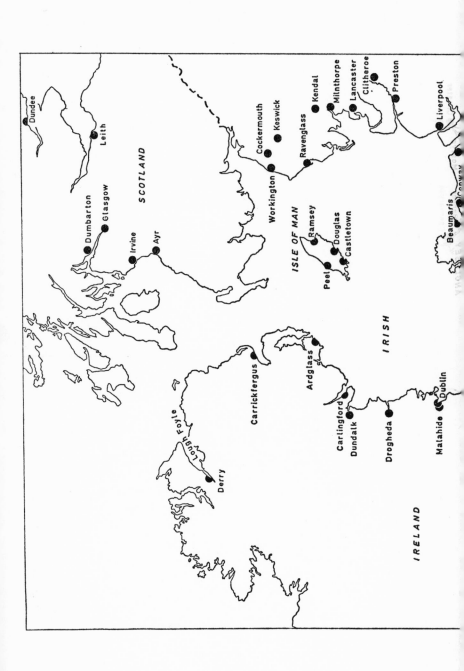

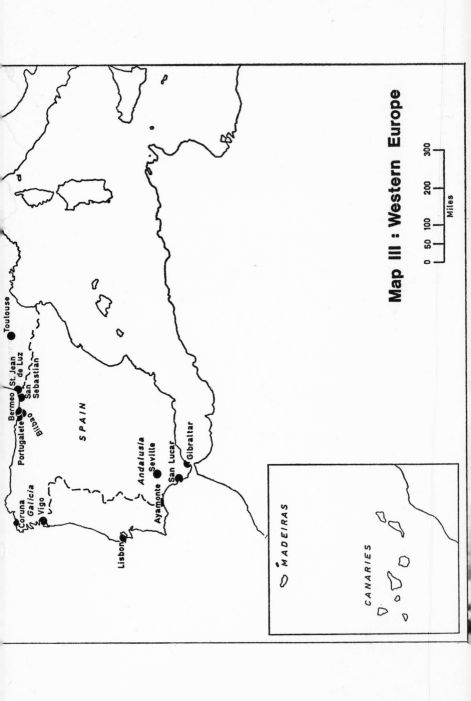

Map III : Western Europe

INDEX

There are not any references to the trade of Chester or of the River Dee. References to the maps are denoted by Roman numerals. All authors referred to in the text are included.